UP THE FEEDER,
DOWN THE 'MOUTH
and
BACK AGAIN

OTHER WORKS BY THE AUTHOR

PLAYS & MUSICALS

THE BLACK MAN (BRISTOL OLD VIC THEATRE SCHOOL, 1965)
HISLOP (HTV, 1969)
THE CHEF (HTV, 1970)
BLACK DEATH (EXETER UNIVERSITY DRAMA DEPARTMENT, 1975)
PROSTITUTES (AVON TOURING COMPANY, 1976)
BATTLE OF BRITAIN (NEW VENTURES, 1977)
FACE VALUE (AVON TOURING COMPANY, 1977)
[IN COLLABORATION WITH TOM STOPPARD] ALBERT'S BRIDGE EXTENDED
(REVUNIONS, 1978)
JOCKEYS AS LIFE (HTV, 1978)
MASTER OF LETTERS (PLAYWRIGHTS COMPANY, 1979)
AUDITION (HTV, 1980)
CHERRY (SOLENT PEOPLE'S THEATRE COMPANY, 1981)
GOD'S WONDERFUL RAILWAY (BRISTOL OLD VIC, 1985)
PERICLES [RECONSTRUCTION OF SHAKESPEARE]
(THEATER EMORY, ATLANTA, 1987; SHOW OF STRENGTH, 1990)
AN EVENING WITH DR GRACE (WESSEX ACTORS COMPANY, 1995)
UP THE FEEDER, DOWN THE 'MOUTH (BRISTOL OLD VIC, 1997)
BREATHLESS HUSH (HTV, 1999)
ALBERT'S BRIDGE, A MUSICAL PLAY (SHAFTESBURY COMMUNITY THEATRE, 1999)

FICTION

THE CROWD (CHAPMAN & HALL, 1965)
ZERO SUMMER (EYRE & SPOTTISWOODE, 1971)
TREATMENT (WEIDENFELD & NICOLSON, 1976)
THE JERICHO GUN (WEIDENFELD & NICOLSON, 1977)
EDWARD & MRS SIMPSON (WEIDENFELD & NICOLSON, 1978)
EXTRA COVER (WEIDENFELD & NICOLSON, 1981)
THE DARK CRYSTAL (JIM HENSON/HOLT, 1982)
WAGNER (HEYNE, 1983)
LADY JANE (WEIDENFELD & NICOLSON, 1985)
SEBASTIAN THE NAVIGATOR (WEIDENFELD & NICOLSON, 1985)
LABYRINTH (JIM HENSON/HOLT, 1986)
THE DANGEROUS MEMOIR OF CITIZEN SADE (LOXWOOD STONELEIGH, 2000)

NON-FICTION

ORGHAST AT PERSEPOLIS (METHUEN, 1972)
PAPER VOICES (CHATTO & WINDUS, 1975)

UP THE FEEDER, DOWN THE 'MOUTH

and
BACK AGAIN

A play about
Bristol Docks

by
A.C.H. Smith

Published by Loxwood Stoneleigh, an imprint of Falling Wall Press
First edition 2001

Designed and typeset by Falling Wall Press Ltd
Printed and bound in Great Britain by Antony Rowe Ltd, Chippenham

Illustrations
Front cover: Photograph courtesy of Port of Bristol Authority Collection at Bristol
    Industrial Museum
Back cover: Members of the Company, June 2001 (photo: g burke photography)

ISBN 1 85135 040 3

Falling Wall Press is grateful for the support of John Adler Associates
in publishing this play.

Falling Wall Press Ltd
225 (Top Floor) Gloucester Road, Bristol BS7 8NR, England

Introduction

The dates of kings and queens and battles, the policies of governments, the causes of wars and alliances and trade agreements – in order to understand history we need to know such things, but they are not the story. They are the frame. The picture within the frame is of the lives that ordinary people led, how they dealt with the conditions that the statesmen, or natural accident, produced. Henry V's speech at Agincourt is fine propaganda. Shakespeare's true story is in the previous scene, the night before the battle, when the king disguises himself in order to move freely among his tense soldiers and hear the concerns of men with names like Bates and Williams. Similarly, television reporters ask people caught up in news events: how did it feel? What happened can usually be pieced together. What we really want to know is what it meant to those involved. Knowing that, we might imagine ourselves going through the experience, and so learn something more useful than facts. And that is what the theatre is best at.

When the Cabot 500 celebrations of 1997 were approaching, the Bristol Old Vic decided that it was a good time to look at what life was like in more recent years, when Bristol was still a busy port, and ships were being loaded and unloaded at the end of the street only a few yards from the theatre. Official histories tell us what happened, for nearly a thousand years. To know what difference it made to the people who lived in the seafaring city and worked in the port or on the ships, you go and ask them, while they are still alive and full of memories, some 20-odd years after the city docks closed. What you get in return are facts and opinions, but above all stories, first-hand or handed down, because a good story tells you what you really want to know. You also come up with a strong draught of the Bristol sense of humour, drier than the sherry they used to unload.

It's no exaggeration to say that you could easily gather the material for 20 different plays about Bristol docks. There are hundreds of people with stories they could tell you. We listened to some 50 men and women, and from all that they told us we selected a sample that seemed to add up to a full picture.

Then, what do you do on stage with all of that? You could choose to invent a dramatic narrative, using the researched material as rich background. We chose to make a different sort of play, in a tradition established in this country by the pre-war Unity Theatre, by Joan Littlewood in east London and Peter Cheeseman in Stoke, and already exploited by the Bristol Old Vic in 1985 in *God's Wonderful Railway*, a small-scale show about the GWR. We would dramatise the stories themselves. Once we had taken that decision, it was our job to set all the stories within a frame, because an audience wants to travel with a journey that begins and ends. There is, in fact, more than one frame. A ship comes in, is unloaded, loaded up again, and steams out. A day's work starts and finishes. A docker reaches the last day of his working life and remembers the first. The city docks is a thriving workplace with its own long history, and it is closed down.

Within that multiple frame, there is room to touch in the shape of a few men's and women's lives. They are lives drawn from those of people we listened to; but because this is a stage play, not a documentary, we have distributed the contents of those lives among a gallery of parts, with the result that no character should be consistently identified with a single, real person.

Nor, though it is a play about a community, should it be described as a community play. That term defines a special kind of production, in which a town or village creates and performs a play in celebration of itself, with input from theatre professionals. Our work went the other way around. We were delighted to be able to stage an unusually big production by enlisting dozens of amateur performers and Youth Theatre members, who served as crowd, chorus, and *corps de ballet*. Their enthusiasm and discipline were exemplary. They are rooted in the community of Bristol, as are all the professional actors in the show.

Andy Hay's 1997 production in the Theatre Royal was received warmly by the people it was staged for, and about. Some 12,000 people saw it. The songs, with music by John O'Hara, were issued as a cassette album, and it sold out. People old enough to remember the city docks were moved and amused. To younger people, it was a revelation to see how the port's business, its smells and noises and sweat and hardships and foreign flavours, once identified the heart of the city – the reason why Bristol is here at all – and to wonder what's left, now that docking is a containerised and distant industry behind guarded gates at Avonmouth and Portbury.

The 2001 revival, staged on the historic waterfront, gives us the opportunity, for once, to benefit from hindsight. A few stories that, during the 1997 run, began to seem distractions from the main thrust have been dropped. Some new ones have been worked in, following more conversations with old port workers. The text printed here is the revised version. It will not be a word-perfect version of what is performed – things always change in the boiler-room of rehearsal. But it will serve as a fairly souvenir of the production.

A.C.H. Smith

THE CHARACTERS

A gang of dockers
MAGICOTE
DOLLY
HAPPY PAPPY
RED BARON
CABBAGE WATER
WHIPPET

HARRY, *sea captain*
SPOT, *prostitute*
MRS Q, *pub landlady.*

Kids
MICK, ANDY, DEREK, PETER (*young* CABBAGE WATER), KIT

Other speaking parts
SIGNALMAN, VICAR, PILOT, WOOLWORTH'S, WHITE WHALE,
STEVEDORE, CRANE DRIVER (*off*), DOCKER 1, DOCKER 2,
COPPER, OLAF, GOD (*off*)

*The Company for the 2001 production
can be found on pages 59-63.*

UP THE FEEDER, DOWN THE 'MOUTH
and BACK AGAIN

Empty dockside. Distant hooter. SPOT/SINGER *enters.*
SONG *(quiet).* She's coming in,
        She's coming in,
        Our ship's coming in ...
    KIDS *enter.* DOCKERS *starting to arrive.*
MICK. What's that one then?
ANDY. A Dan.
PETER. No.
ANDY. Dan, bet you. Gurt red'un.
PETER. No. Bristol Steam, that is.
ANDY. What does thee know?
SONG. She's coming in,
        She's coming in,
        Our ship's coming in ...
MAGICOTE. When I say goodbye in the mornings I can't bear to look
    at her eyes. Not knowing if there'll be any work for me today.
    Hoot, slightly closer. HARRY *will become visible on bridge of ship.*
DOLLY. I said goodbye to my missus this morning for the last time.
HAPPY PAPPY. What? You don't think you'll last the day out?
DOLLY. I'm finishing. This is it. I get my pension tomorrow.
RED BARON. One more job for someone else.
SONG. She's coming with tinned meat and cherry brandy,
        Cattle-cake and bulbs of gladioli.
CABBAGE. Gladioli – few of those come out the sack, they'll do
    nicely in me garden.
SONG. Pears in syrup, timber, grain, soap, fridges,
        Sugared raisins ...
KIDS. All right.
SONG. ... macaroni.
KIDS. Macaroni – ugh!
SONG. Wood pulp for St. Anne's goes up the Feeder,
        Past the Midland Wharf and Netham Lock.
        Sherry, sugar, cattle, coming in,
        From all across the world to Bristol dock.
        Look at the flags! They are flying.

Look at the flags blowing free.
(Two hoots.) Pay day.
RED BARON. Yeh, it's pay day so long as you got blue eyes.
SONG. She's coming in with trade –
HAPPY PAPPY. She's coming in with rats. You see tarpaulins rippling
– thousands of rats under it.
DOLLY. Hey son, you haven't got your yorks on.
ROBIN. What's yorks, then?
DOLLY *(points to his)*. Stops the rats running up your legs.
MAGICOTE. And you got your hobnails to squelch 'em.
MICK. I knew that.
HAPPY PAPPY. I'll teach you something you don't know. See those
men there come from Bedminster Down? In the old days they'd
have worn red sweat rags round their necks. You come from
Parson Street, a green one. Different gangs, see? Yellow, blue.
There, you've learned something today. Now go to school. Go
on, bugger off. It's time.
SONG. The floating Harbour's always full on Mondays –
Ships tied up abreast, some weeks, they are.
All around The Ostrich and Welsh Back,
Both sides down to Hotwells, up the Centre.
Look at the flags! They are flying.
Look at the flags blowing free.
Look at the flags, they are flying.
Look at the flags blowing free.
Footage of our ship / archive.
HARRY. You've waited for the tide in Walton Bay.
A captain can get fidgety, working out
The moment to weigh anchor, and go up
So Hotwells lock is ready to receive us.
It's an exciting river. You get no help
From the port to find your way up. Signalmen
At Avonmouth, Shirehampton or Sea Mills
Might signal that a ship is coming down.
SIGNALMAN *(pointing)*. Watch yourself!
HARRY. We pick up a pilot, and hobblers in case ropes might be
needed on shore. In the pilots' watch-house at Pill, they see us
coming round Nelson Point, and by the time we near the old
Custom House they are out in their boat. On the big spring tides,

if the wind's nor'west you can get a six-foot sea run in that stretch. Dark winter's night, no lights, the pilot has to judge it so fine. She's coming in four or five knots. She can't slow down – we know our time margin. The stop gates go on at about an hour to flow. If you miss them, you can't get through until the ebb tide, perhaps three or four o'clock in the morning. We local men, we know we'll be home for bedtime if the pilot comes from Pill.

VICAR. Pill is famous for stupid, brutal, abandoned wickedness.

HARRY. Nevertheless, we do understand the river. It goes back 500 years, when ships were towed up and down by rowing boats, or horses. The flow can sweep a ship crosswise onto the mud banks, and if it's stuck, at low tide it will crack its hull. If you're going to miss the tide, you're safer if you get yourself hung up on the high banks at Hung Road. In the old days, while they were waiting there for the tide, a minister used to preach to them.

VICAR. Peace be upon you. And keep away from Pill.

WHIPPET *has entered, holding a black book.*

HAPPY PAPPY. You look lost, lad. You new?

WHIPPET. Yeh. I got my black book.

DOLLY. You're all right, then. Where did you get that from?

WHIPPET. My Dad.

DOLLY. It's always the same, father to son. Who was he, your Dad?

WHIPPET. Whippet. That's what they called him, Whippet.

DOLLY *(to* KIDS*).* Hey, you, hop it. You're not allowed in here.

MICK. There ain't no gates.

DOLLY. No, but there's custom and practice in the port area. And if that's not enough for you, there's the back of my hand for kids who give me lip. *(*KIDS *exit.)*

HARRY. The bow-man claps onto our rope, the pilot climbs aboard, takes the wheel, and away we go, towing the boat alongside. Ahead of you there's some tobacco barges. The pilot asks if you agree we'd better get past them, or we'll be late getting up the river. Agreed. Telegraph to: Increase Speed. *(Puts telegraph over.)* After Pill, it's rocky on the Somerset side, but the deeper water lies there so we surge past the rocks as close as we dare, closer than comfortable when an outward-bound ship is hogging the river. Past Chapel Pill, the Powder House is the start of Horseshoe Bend.

MAGICOTE. Horseshoe Bend attracts fog. It rolls up the river with the flood tide. The visibility once was down to a few feet. Ship after ship went aground. The river was blocked for weeks.

HAPPY PAPPY. One foggy night there's a crew who abandon their ship, the Peri, on the mud. But they forget to anchor her out, look, and now the tide's come up and floated her off. And they're rowing around in the fog –

HAPPY PAPPY & DOLLY *(miming rowers, call)*. You seen the Peri anywhere?

CABBAGE. Another wreck, it had a piano on board. These rascals think, we'll liberate 'ee. So they gets it on their boat and they're rowing it over to Rownham, but they run into some coppers, out checking. So all they can do is pull the plug and scuttle the boat. And the piano comes floating up river.

DOLLY. When the Ettrick capsized, everyone in Pill had a new pair of boots! And we kids done pretty well with chocolates.

MAGICOTE. After the Kron Prinz sinks, it takes weeks to salvage her. So the Port and Pier Railway, alongside the river there, they show some Bristol enterprise, don't they? They throws up a temporary station there so passengers can alight and get a proper *view* of the disaster.

HAPPY PAPPY. Nowadays, with radar, it's supposed to be safer. The maritime insurance people have brought in a new classification of accident: radar-assisted collisions.

HARRY. Coming under the Suspension Bridge, the green light on the signal mast tells you if the locks are ready for you. The hobblers get in their boat and sheer off to the slipway, to be on the quay to take our ropes. The public convenience is a landmark where masters often run a bow-rope out to help the ship round the port-hand turn into the locks.

PILOT. Bring up at the piss-house!

SONG. She's coming in ...
  She's coming in ...
  Our ship's coming in ...

CABBAGE. Whippet's lad, are you?

WHIPPET. When he give me his book, he said, here, look after it like it's gold.

CABBAGE. Keep your wits about you. Just watch, and do what we do.

MAGICOTE. There's two and a half thousand of us to watch, here and down the 'Mouth. Should be enough.

RED BARON. Yes. But that means there's two and a half thousand men after the same job as you are. It's all friendly enough here now, waiting. Once he's up on that stand at a quarter to eight, you're on your own, sonny.

WHIPPET *makes aggressive gesture.*

HAPPY PAPPY. Easy lad, steady now, save it – you'll need it later on.

WHIPPET. I'm just looking to earn a living, that's all.

HAPPY PAPPY. That's all any of us wants.

RED BARON. You'll get a good living if you lick somebody's arse.

DOLLY *(in* WHIPPET'*s ear).* Him there, that's Red Baron, that is. That's what we calls him, Red Baron. He's a militant, see. What that means is that he's fierce, terrible fierce, in standing up for dockers' rights. But don't ask him to do any work. He won't be interested in that. You'd offend him.

WHIPPET. Red Baron.

DOLLY. Always stirring it he is.

WHIPPET. You ought to call him Spoon, then.

DOLLY. Red Baron, that's what he's called. Always stirring it. There's plenty to stir about, oh yes, you wait. But there's ways to do it.

WHIPPET. Through the Union.

Laughter.

CABBAGE. The Union! Oh dear. And you a docker's son.

RED BARON. I'll tell you how it is, lad, working here. Go to the Nelson on Redcliffe Hill on a Sunday, the stevedore's waiting there for you to buy him a pint, you'll get work Monday. Or leave beer in the club. Take the boss home in your car and make a five-mile detour. Or join the docks rowing club. Ten per cent of dockers earn really good money. They're blue eyes. Ninety per cent dive in the pig bin. Me, I've never touched my forelock. If I think something is wrong, logically and legitimately, I speak my word. And for this, I am branded. The stevedores have been instructed not to pick up militants like me. They call me a wrecker. That's the insidious word they use.

CABBAGE. To get yourself established with an employer, you've got to do everything he offers you. He expects the men that get their living from him to do the harder work. It's easy to fall out of line with him. And then next morning you stand, and the six men around you get the job, and you don't.

HAPPY PAPPY. He's got his son and his son-in-law and his friends, all in the gang. He picks up the same six holdsmen and one man on the top. The Easy Six. They're his blue-eyes.

SONG. Blue eyes, blue eyes, you're one of the gang,
      And the stevedore tells all the rest to go hang.
      Blue eyes, blue eyes, you'll never be poor,
      Not with a boss for a father-in-law.

RED BARON. Cruel, hard-eyed men they are. You'll never see them at a strike meeting. But, they can graft, I'll say that. They know how to do it. They're a team. They won't have nobody carried.

DOLLY. The thing is, they cut corners, do things that are not right. I've been to the Union office over them. And all that happens is, they gets a reprimand and I get left out, on the stones. They go all the way round you purposely. Because you complained. You don't have to complain.

MAGICOTE. Your stevedore, he can make you or break you. It's like the Mafia. You can't get a job if your face don't fit.

SONG. Blue eyes, blue eyes, your eyes are so blue,
      The stevedore's taken a fancy to you.
      Blue eyes, blue eyes, much bluer than mine,
      Why don't you bend over and let the sun shine?

CABBAGE. You have a stevedore walks around the deck. A foreman, a hatch foreman to each hatch you go to . The superintendent, the assistant superintendent, the shed foreman. You have more bosses on the quay than anything.

HAPPY PAPPY. And between the lot of them they know nothing. Nothing.

CABBAGE as STEVEDORE. Go down the sharp end ...

HAPPY PAPPY. Even after 10 years, he still can't think to call it the bow.

CABBAGE as STEVEDORE. Go down the sharp end. There's a group of they Indian officers down there. The one thee wants is the engineer. Thee casn't miss him, he got a turbine on his head.

MAGICOTE. But they're all down there, strutting around. Especially for overtime. Even if there's only one gang working, they all come down then. Everybody makes money.

HARRY. If you approach the locks with a spring tide rushing up astern and find all the berths occupied, and a procession of ships leaving the basin, you back and fill, trying to keep on the Hotwells side to give the outgoing ships a passage. Then you've got to get into that narrow lock, just two inches' clearance on the biggest ships, or you'll be carried past, and you could run aground and need a tug.

HAPPY PAPPY. When a steam tug appears on the River Avon – 30 years after they'd become normal in other docks, mind – the boatmen of Pill are quick to grasp how effective it will be. So a gang of them goes out and tries to scuttle it.

CABBAGE. Tugs, huh. I seen one, it pulls a ship off the mud so sudden, the tug shoots back and grounds. Then the ship has to pull *it* off. That might go on a long time, that.

DOLLY. Eh, Young Whippet. When you're coming up there in a thick fog, how do you know when you've got to turn into Hotwells lock?

WHIPPET. When you're coming up there in a thick fog, how do you know when you've got to turn into Hotwells lock?

DOLLY. Simple. You keep singing out: 'Men of Harlech …'

MAGICOTE. Piss off home, you Welsh bastard!

DOLLY. Then you know you're at Hotwells.

HARRY. In the basin, we wait for our turn to enter the Floating Harbour. The basin is ringed with pubs. Turn your back and the crew are gone. If they don't come running when you sound your whistle you have to search The Pilot, Nova Scotia, Merchant's Arms …

DOLLY. The Ship, The General Draper, Rownham Hotel, The Gloster, Swansea Arms, Rose of Denmark, Dowry Hotel, York Hotel, The Bear, Steam Packet, The Albion, The Globe – what comes next?

SPOT. The Spring Gardens.

DOLLY. Spring Gardens, Dock Gate Tavern, Plume of Feathers, Mardyke Hotel, The Juno, Suspension Bridge Tavern, Crown and Anchor, American Eagle, Myrtle Tree, another Albion, Three Tuns …

CABBAGE. I see this pair outside The Ostrich, after a session on the Black Knight – they'd both got these pocket watches on a chain,

15

right, and they was playing conkers with 'em.

HARRY. The harbour takes a gentle S bend past Canon's Marsh, with the vast GWR marshalling yards behind, and Wapping and Railway Wharves to starboard. We are nearing the heart of the port. Give the signal.

SONG. She's coming in …
She's coming in …
Our ship's coming in …

HARRY. And all the time we're performing this intricate manoeuvre of docking, the harbour pilot is rabbiting: "Port five … Midships … No, captain, you will find that the best underpants you can buy, starboard five, are Marks and Spencer's. For years now, midships, my wife has been buying mine there, port five, and she's washed 'em and washed 'em, midships, and they're still, I can't say as good as new, starboard 10, slow ahead, but perfectly respectable, not a hole to be seen in 'em, midships, steady as she goes, and she wouldn't think of buying them anywhere else, stop engines."

Four blasts of ship's hooter. The doors are opened, to reveal a ship docking

SONG. Three blasts mean she's coming in on starboard,
Engines go astern to bring her in.
Four blasts say she's turning to come port side,
Ready for the next trip to begin.

Twice a day the tide fills up the gorge.
Twice a day there's work if you can find it.
Our ship's coming in, we hope – but pray
Another ship will follow in behind it.

Elder Dempster, Libby, Clan, and Blue Star,
Bristol City and BSNC,
Geest, the Dans, Black Star, Nigerian National,
Coming in from all across the sea.

Look at the flags, they are flying –
Four corners of the earth
Crossing the seas and tying
Up in a Bristol berth.

Look at the flags, they are flying,
Look at the flags blowing free,

Look at the flags, they are flying,
Look at the flags blowing free.

The DOCKERS *turn and run from the ship into the Pen. Archive footage of Pen. Doors close.* STEVEDORE *appears on platform. Hubbub.* DOCKERS *crush forward holding their books up. They try to help* WHIPPET *understand.*

DOLLY. When he has a job he knows his own people won't like, he takes the ones from the front.

HAPPY PAPPY. He knows which gang to put on certain cargoes. They're specialists.

MAGICOTE. Yeh, specialists at holding a 10-shilling note up with their book to get the cream pitch. Or slipping their book under someone else's when it's handed up, so he's taken it before he knows. Slimy moves like that.

CABBAGE. Then all that's left is the oranges or potatoes, that kind of crap, cockles, that hardly pays anything. Sweeping up the shed. When they call for a scab job like that we stay at the back of the pen, but he'll come after you.

HAPPY PAPPY *as STEVEDORE.* Come on, come on, all books in. Let's have your books.

MAGICOTE. It's degrading, only men's got to suffer it. You got to make yourself available for work.

DOLLY. We call it the screw. Some mornings, perhaps 50 go to work. The other 550 don't.

HAPPY PAPPY *as STEVEDORE.* It's just unfortunate, you have to leave men out.

CABBAGE. I've seen them so desperate and clawing at him for work they've pulled his trousers off. Always lots of laughs in here. I mean, you wouldn't bring your mother in. I never do.

RED BARON. In the pen, all friendship ceases. Blokes you play skittles with, it means nothing.

DOLLY. Stand up on your toes, poke your neck up and puff your chest out and hope he'll give you a job.

RED BARON. You get pushed over, you'll be trampled. There's men had their legs broke.

HAPPY PAPPY. And immediately you hand up your book and you've got work, the employer becomes your enemy.

RED BARON. The Lords of Life and Death. Like the emperors of Rome, who could see no wrong. Hands behind their backs.

MAGICOTE. The clerk who collects the books, he's only a kid. I doubt if he can believe it. That men are crushing forward, trying to get their books into his hands so they'll have a job today.

RED BARON. You seen that film *Zulu*? You don't need to. Just come in here every morning.

SONG. When you go in the Pen
    You got six hundred men
    All wanting work, shoving, hustling.
    The stevedores prod
    And a few get the nod,
    Bought on the hoof, prime muscle.
    And the rest get the bump,
    Like a brand on the rump,
    Dumped on the stones, nothing to do.
    We're screwing for pay,
    Same every day,
    On the screw.

CABBAGE. We never hold up our books. He knows what our gang can do.

MAGICOTE. The hands go up and he just collects 'em, the first books he can reach. It's as damn stupid as that. The others get the green stamp. They call it the bump.

HAPPY PAPPY. If you're bumped, you sit around and perhaps have a cup of tea. You got no work. If there's a tide, you can try again at dinner-time.

SONG. And the rest get the bump,
    Like a brand on the rump,
    Dumped on the stones, nothing to do.
    We're screwing for pay,
    Same every day,
    We're screwing for pay,
    Same every day,
    On the screw.

Hubbub rises again. And fades. Doors open. A lorry is to be loaded from the ship.

DOLLY. The bosses don't really have any control over how quickly the job gets done. If he comes along and says, "What are you doing down there?", he'll be told politely where to go. Fred Reed, that's the easiest firm to work for. They're proper simple, they are. Proper daft.

CABBAGE. You call the bosses by their first name. And they call you by your name, or your nickname. You'll get one.

MAGICOTE. We'll have to call you something. Give it time.

DOLLY. Everyone's got a nickname, and there's always a story to it. Like there's Broken Boomerang. He never comes back.

CABBAGE. Underpants. Always on the bum, he is.

HAPPY PAPPY. Oh yes. Look – over in that gang you got Man In A Suitcase.

WHIPPET. Eh?

MAGICOTE. He lives in Downend, see, so he tells his wife he's an engineer. He leaves for work in a suit, brings his overalls in a suitcase, when he gets here he changes into them.

CABBAGE. The Destroyer – he's always after a sub.

HAPPY PAPPY. We had a lot of cockneys come down when the war was on. They see this chap who's lost half an ear, they dub him Eighteen Months. Year and a half.

CABBAGE (*producing things from his pockets*). Want to buy a pencil? Pair of shoelaces? Packet of geranium seeds?

MAGICOTE. Walking Woolworth's –

WHITE WHALE. They calls me the White Whale. Blowed if I know why.

DOLLY. So come on, you're going to work here, here's your first test. What do we call the bloke who never goes out?

WHIPPET. I dunno.

DOLLY. The Olympic Flame. You've got a lot to learn. Me, I'm Dolly. Bert Gray, so – Dolly Gray, right?

HAPPY PAPPY. Not for much longer.

DOLLY. When I started they used to call me Splinter, that was me, Splinter, because there wasn't two penn'orth of me.

MAGICOTE. You could have thrown him over the side with no splash.

DOLLY. But in the army I put a bit on.

HAPPY PAPPY. Me, I lost a stone, in the desert.

MAGICOTE. Trust you to lose a stone in a desert.

CABBAGE. The only thing I lost in the army was my innocence.

MAGICOTE. You soon found it again.

DOLLY. Now him there, he's Magicote – one coat covers everything, see.

MAGICOTE. And that's Happy Pappy, father of seven. Or is it eight?

HAPPY PAPPY. Can't remember. That one, he's Cabbage Water. He drinks it to get strong.

CABBAGE. Bit of vinegar on it, don't taste that bad.

MAGICOTE, Young Whippet. That'll do for now. You'll get a name of your own soon enough, once you give your game away.

HAPPY PAPPY. Like one you'll meet, we calls him Muscles. A proper nut, he is. Thinks he's some kind of Tarzan.

WHIPPET. Why don't you call him Tarzan, then?

HAPPY PAPPY. We've already got a Tarzan. You'll be arguing about athletes, say, how they start, and his little ears prick up, and he's at it. I've never seen a man carry four bunches of bananas, but old Muscles will have a go. Dead serious about it, he is.

DOLLY. That's the worst job on the dock, the bananas. The next worse in my idea is anything to do with a shovel. Shovelling concentrate.

MAGICOTE. Iron ore, sets like an anvil.

HAPPY PAPPY. Carbon black, that's bad stuff.

CABBAGE. And potash.

RED BARON. You have to shovel all that, see, down the hold. But there's one fellow, only little he is, not more than six or seven stone soaking wet by the look of him, he'll work at the main hatch all day and night with a banjo, 24 hours, never stops. The Golden Shoveller, we calls him. There's men take 10 years off their lives, the way they'll slave for money, chasing the buck. I tipped on this infamous red-ore boat. It's hot, it's stinking, it gets into your veins, into your pores. Two weeks afterwards, you wake up with a red-ore sheet.

CABBAGE. The sulphur boat, there's one that canes you. Go down that hold, you can't work with a mask on, because of the heat, so you're breathing in sulphur.

HAPPY PAPPY. You're bearing the brunt of it then.

CABBAGE. Ammonia. Phosphates.

HAPPY PAPPY. What *is* a brunt?

MAGICOTE. After you finish you can have a shower if you want it. But they are anquidated, and the time you mess around having a shower, you could be home and sit in a tin bath. So you come home red, you come home black, covered in flour, or coal dust. These ships that come from the Far East with rice bran, there's thousands of weevils. They nestle in the seams of your trousers. You're sat on the bus and they'll be crawling all over your neck. (*Slaps neck.*)

HAPPY PAPPY (*as lady, ringing bus bell*). Let me off at the next stop. Those men are lousy.

MAGICOTE. You bring it all home. Wet hides.

CABBAGE (*as wife*). Comes home smelling of wet hides.

MAGICOTE. I can't even smell it.

RED BARON. The Turkish ship. Up to there in water. Turds, Turkish turds, floating about on the water. Down in the hold they're saying, "Oi, oi, it ain't good enough, it ain't good enough." And I say, "Out of it. When you've cleared that up and disinfected it, we'll go back to work down there." I don't ask for the moon.

CABBAGE. He would if he thought it might stir up trouble.

HAPPY PAPPY. We've screwed extra out of them for one or two jobs. Sugar, you get sticky all over. They give us sixpence extra for that. It's called sticky money. And after D-Day, there was stiff money.

WHIPPET. Uh?

HAPPY PAPPY. There were coffins being shipped home through the docks with dead Americans in 'em. Handling those we'd get paid stiff money, it was called.

DOLLY. And for timber you get a shilling extra. Splinter money, that is.

MAGICOTE. There's always a timber boat tied up. Scandinavia or Russia, they come from.

DOLLY. It lasts a week or two, discharging a cargo of timber. Deal running, it's called. The ship winches it over the side, and you pick it up, 12 to 15 long planks, and carry it over into the pile. You have a leather saddle. But an old uncle used to live in the same house as me, he ran timber, and I've seen him come home and all the blood running out of a sore on the back of his head big as a cup. It rubs and rubs, where your shoulder ain't used to it. But I found a way. I take her silk underskirts in. Widdle on it, stick it in there, and that's fine then.

Lorry drives off.

HAPPY PAPPY. Tea break.

A distant hoot. On dockside, CABBAGE *is clearing up stuff.* KIDS *enter.* ANDY *is sniffing the air.*

DEREK. What is it?

MICK. Sugared raisins?

ANDY. No ... Cork. *(Sniffs.)* Cheese. Tobacco.

DEREK *groans.*

MICK. No sugared raisins?

CABBAGE. Oi, you lot.

DEREK. He looks like that pirate with his hook.

CABBAGE. You shouldn't be to here.

KIT. And you should be hanging from Prince Street Bridge.

MICK. Head down.

ROBIN. Yeh, so the tide comes up and drowns you. That's what they does to pirates.

ANDY *sniffs.*

MICK. Sugared raisins?

ANDY. No. Peanuts.

DEREK. Peanuts don't smell.

Peanuts hit ground, and KIDS *scatter, except for* PETER, *who has been gazing up at the ship, and has now gone halfway up the gangway.*

PETER. What do they do to a stowaway when they catch him?

HARRY. It's up to them. Make him walk the plank, if they want. You shouldn't be here.

SONG. When you have had it up to here,
        You can't afford a pint of beer,
        Your head's gone down, your shoulders slump,
        What do you do? The pierhead jump.

        When you've just got to get away,
        Can't stand it here another day,
        You're out of luck, you've got the hump,
        What do you do? The pierhead jump.

CABBAGE. That was me. I did the pierhead jump.

WHIPPET. What, were you running away?

CABBAGE. No, I wasn't running away. My home life was idyllic. Sea Mills, we spent all our time on the river. It's just – I was going into the Navy anyway, in a few months when I was 15 and a half, but I couldn't wait. I had an office-boy job at Avonmouth, and I spent all my lunchtimes out there on the dock, looking at the ships. Moored up at the oil jetty was an American tanker, the Hanging Rock. The opportunity arose and I took it.

PETER. When you sailing?

[Underlining: CABBAGE does voice of PURSER]

CABBAGE. On the 2.30 tide. *(Aside)* It's now or never. Have you got any Popeye comics, please, mister? Sure. Wait there. And when his back's turned, I nip up the gangway. *(PETER does so.)* I don't even know where we're going. I hide in this locker, then in a lifeboat. I've got nothing with me to eat or drink. After three nights, I give myself up. I knock on the door of the wheelhouse, very apprehensive I am. He opens it. I'm a stowaway. I want to give myself up. *(Laughing)* God damn, we've got a Limey stowaway. They are great. They radio back that they've discovered me, then give me a huge meal, which I bring up over the side. The food is amazing. I mean it's 1946, we're still rationed. They have everything you ever wanted. Beef, pork, lamb, chicken, turkey, icecream, Coca Cola, as much coffee as you can drink. Now we've got a job for you, Peggy. That's what they call you when you're the youngest member of the crew – the Peggy. Don't ask me. Mess boy. Over to Curaçao, back across to Dakar, then Aruba, in the Dutch West Indies. Then they're sent back to Avonmouth, fortunately for me. Altogether a month and a half. Much later, after Dad died, in his papers I found a letter.

HARRY *as PURSER (reads).* Dear Mrs Silk, I am Peter's acting mother. I've reprimanded him or patted his back when he had it coming. It's been a grand experience for him, and frankly for all of us. We have been exposed to a magician – the magic of "Thank you very much", "If you will, please", "Excuse me", and a few gross of similar shortcuts to men's hearts. He'll return to you laden with stories which always come with one's first trip to sea. Slowly, he will begin to elaborate on them. These months have been good investments for him, but they will never justify the anguish you must have gone through. I can promise he will be cognisant of that. I want to compliment you on the splendid job you have done in providing Peter with the foundation of character on which to build his life, even though the odds were stacked against you ...

CABBAGE. I think he was referring to the war, not to me.

HARRY *as PURSER (reads).* Be concerned about Peter, but don't worry.

SONG. When you've just got to get away,
     Can't stand it here another day,
     You're out of luck, you've got the hump,
     What do you do? The pierhead jump.

     Far away places,
     With magnetic names,
     Caracas, Odessa,
     Macao, Conakry,
     There's a place for you and me ...
     Worse things happen at sea ...

     No place like home. You come ashore,
     But it's no place to be once more.
     It's worse than before, you're down with a bump,
     So what do you do? The pierhead jump.

   Hooter. Underscored canon begins at point to be decided. Banana unloading starts.

STEVEDORE. Let's have you, then. Bid ends aft!

HAPPY PAPPY. Only 25 million to go.

MAGICOTE. But look up at the ship. Magnificent.

HAPPY PAPPY. The only thing worse than discharging a skin boat is being down in its bowels, shovelling coal, all the way to America and back.

MAGICOTE. For the passengers it's the Rolls Royce of shipping. Gleaming white. Magnificent.

HAPPY PAPPY. The engine room. The black gang.

MAGICOTE. The Cavina, the Bayano, Carare, Camito, Ariguani.

HAPPY PAPPY. It's Dante's Inferno. You go down from the fiddly through a little cast-iron door, with steel dogs on. Clamber over the top of the coal stack – about a foot clearance under the deckhead. Get to where the open hatch is. Then you shovel the coal from the hatch, and gradually shovel your way back to the entrance. That's your first thing, making your way, so you can get out. Every time the ship moves all the coal moves.

MAGICOTE. The teak rails polished, paint glistening.

HAPPY PAPPY. Fire doors open, red hot clinker, steaming ashes, orange glow on the sweating bodies. Unlaced boots, oil-stained bib and brace, sweat rag, woollen longjohns, elbow-length vest.

MAGICOTE. The courtesy flag flying from the foretopmast, denoting the West Indies. On the starboard yardarm your Blue Peter, on the port yardarm the Royal Mail pennant. Everything correct and proper. Look at the luggage labels – you're carrying the aristocracy of England, sat up on the boat deck.

HAPPY PAPPY. Four hours shovelling. In the coal stack, the light is magnificent – an old oil can, with a piece of rope stuck down the spout. A naked flame, that's your light. There's always coffee on. Black, like treacle. Keeps you going.

MAGICOTE. You come home loaded with 25 million bananas.

(Shouts) Remember your first-class passengers are the bananas.

HAPPY PAPPY. They have to be kept at 53 degrees. Between the ship's side and the banana pens there's alleys on each deck. It's the job of an ordinary seaman to go down every day and crawl through reading the temperatures with a torch. When I hear, "Oh, I found a tarantula in the bananas" – we see dozens of 'em. Snakes, banana rats. Once the refrigerating plant is started, all your rats down in the hold come up into the quarters. And you've never seen rats like it. They're as big as cats, banana rats. You kill 'em with anything you have – hammer, bucket, spanner, anything. We've got a ship's cat, but he can't ... It's impossible. A cat is a mighty king of the world, though. I've seen ships' cats in a foreign port wander along the quayside, and tom up, and come back on board as proud as punch. Yeh, and I don't suppose the bastard had ever been there before! The cat, he's everyone's friend, the only bit of humanity you have.

MAGICOTE. Remember your first-class passengers are the bananas.

STEVEDORE. Big ends aft, men.

SONG. Skin boats are bringing
    Green ripes and plantains,
    Musa sapientiums,
    Grass mitchells.
    Big ends aft now men.
    Before they yellow they're

First Class passengers,
Atlantic swells.

STEVEDORE. Big ends aft, men!

DOLLY. Most of us try and get clear of the banana boats. It's boring, just walking up and down, up and down, 250 men up and down. Four decks. The bottom deck's the worst, because all the mess falls down there. And it's humid. All sorts of things crawling around.

HAPPY PAPPY. After my last time on a banana boat I said, Never again.

SPOT. When Bristol men say Never they mean, definitely not till the week after next.

STEVEDORE. Big ends aft, men!

WHIPPET *with stem of bananas.*

MAGICOTE. Hey, Young Whippet. There's summat just behind 'ee with more legs than thee's got.

WHIPPET *thinks he sees tarantula.*

CABBAGE. You can't drop it. He sees that, you'll get done.

STEVEDORE. Big ends aft, men!

DOLLY. The Lord Mayor comes down and they give him a hand of bananas. Next day, there's a racket out on the dock. One of the girls they employed there at that time – number snatchers we called them; they'd put the labels in the trucks, for their destinations ñ one of them, she's picked up a banana and is eating it. And a couple of kiddies, they're eating 'em. And this policeman arrests 'em. They're no good, they're just ripe bananas. They send the ones just turning ripe to the hospitals. The other ripes, the spotted bananas, which is the best way to have a banana, they only get throwed away anyway, look. And they takes them down the police station. As soon as the chaps hear that – "Right, that's finished. If the Lord Mayor can come down and eat a banana, so can them." And this copper says, "I'm supposed to prosecute them, because they're stealing." Well then, you prosecute them and the bananas can stop there and rot. The one who arrested 'em, he was a bit officious. He was new, yeah, he was new. Later on, when we knew he was behind a wall, we pelted him over the top with frozen green bananas. Like stones, they are. You get a few like him, young and keen. One from Hotwells, I went to

school with him, ugh, he's a heller. You know, he even booked his
father for smoking, on the docks – had his father fined 12 pound!

MAGICOTE. It takes a new copper a while to learn the job. When
they know the ropes they can look down into the hold and see
what we're up to, and turn their back when we comes up. So say if
we take some lemonade bottles down to fill up with whisky or
sherry, brandy, whatever we can tap and reseal, he knows he'll get
some of it later.

HAPPY PAPPY. There was a report of drugs concealed under the hull
of a banana boat. So all the PCs jump in the van, on their way to
the docks they climb into their diving gear, when they get there,
out they swoop – and by now the ship's up in the air on dry dock.

MUSCLES *staggers across with four stems of bananas.*

WHIPPET. That Muscles, he gives it a go all right, don't he?

STEVEDORE. Big ends aft, men!

SONG. Skin boats are bringing
    Green ripes and plantains,
    Musa sapientiums,
    Grass mitchells.
    Big ends aft now men.
    Before they yellow they're
    First Class passengers,
    Atlantic swells.

Docks hooter.

CRANE DRIVER *(off).* That's the one. Dinner-time.

All work stops. GANG *move towards pub.*

CABBAGE. You coming with us over to the pub? Have a Guinness or
six? Talk about the Rovers?

WHIPPET. Who?

CABBAGE. You City, then? I only watch the City during Lent.

WHIPPET. Can we get something to eat?

CABBAGE. What we do is, we bring in a bit of bread and butter, find
a stack of ham, or cheese, or corned beef, the case is just
cardboard, a quick Canadian cut, and *(whistle).* You eat off the
dock. That's the way we does it here.

Pub. MRS Q, HARRY, COPPER, DOCKERS 1 & 2.

MRS Q. No luck today?

DOCKER 1. We got bumped again.

27

HARRY. Four pounds a week for doing nothing.

MRS Q. Yeah, and out of that they stop insurance and tax, if you're paying tax, so you never have much to come at all.

HARRY. Why not try your luck at Avonmouth? You might get four weeks' work there. Or is that why you don't fancy it? ·

DOCKER 2. On what?

The GANG *are entering.*

HARRY. Tomorrow the manganese ship comes in, from Salonika.

MRS Q. They don't call it Salonika, they calls it Thessaloniki.

CABBAGE. Speak Greek do you, Mrs Q?

MRS Q. Speak everything, in here 20 years. I see men come and go. Hear everything here, you do. Except the truth. I don't hear much of that.

RED BARON. I came across a Greek word in a book I was reading.

CABBAGE. Ask Mrs Q.

RED BARON. I could draw it for you, but I read the translation underneath. It meant a sense of shame. And it ran through my mind about the Pen. I thought, there you are, we've all got a sense of shame, every one of us, even the employer.

DOLLY. Eh, Young Whippet. If you're going to be working here, you might as well have a drink with us. I'll square it with Mrs Q. Her and me, we're like that *(gesture)*.

MRS Q. Hey, you. I know how old you are. You live on our street..

DOLLY. Oh, Mrs Q, come on. He's starting as a docker.

MRS Q. One more word out of you and it's goodbye Dolly Gray. Get it?

DOLLY. Got it.

MRS Q. Good *(to* WHIPPET*)*. A half-pint of shandy, I'll serve you that, since you've been on thirsty work. *(To* COPPER*)* What you looking at, then?

COPPER. Amazing how fast they grow up, ain't it?

MRS Q. What amazes me is how they stop growing up once they're 16. That's what I has in here, a blooming gang of teenagers every day, some of them 60 years of age, and been round the world 10 times.

HARRY. Have you ever been abroad, Mrs Q?

MRS Q. Yes. I took the ferry over to Pill once.

MAGICOTE. You watch the Gas last week, Pappy?

HAPPY PAPPY. No. My own lot had a match.

MAGICOTE. You were lucky. A bloke stood behind me got it right. "They'll be talking about this match in the pubs of Bristol for 10 minutes."

MRS Q. Men.

DOLLY. I beg your pardon?

MRS Q. I said Men. All right?

DOLLY. It's your pub.

MRS Q. No, no, I like to think of it as belonging to all of us who enjoy the use of it, just so long as you pay me for what you drink, stick to my rules, and don't question anything I says, all right, Dolly?

DOLLY. Right, right. She goes on like a two-bob watch.

CABBAGE. You'd have made a great stevedore, Mrs Q. You've got the tongue for it.

MRS Q. Is that all it takes?

RED BARON. Too true it is. All tongue, that's what they are.

MRS Q. I've had bosses drinking in here before now.

HAPPY PAPPY. Yeh. Did you ever see one of them with any pockets?

SPOT (entering). I've been so busy today. Up and down gangways on 10 ships.

MRS Q. Oh, your poor feet.

HARRY. When they had her up in court, she told the judge, "You've been round my place too."

HARRY. Sometimes they're waiting dockside in a taxi, with their clothes off ready. Or they try getting on board dressed up as sailors, only they've never got the right shoes. But that can cause confusion among some of the PCs. See a pair of high heels, often enough it's one of the lads of the night.

CABBAGE. Avonmouth, where men are men, and so are some of the women.

SPOT. I've got on board, often enough. Once I was well hidden away when the ship was about to leave. And there's me thinking, mmm, I've always fancied an ocean cruise. And I won't be short of work for a few weeks. So what happens is, this chap I'm with – he's a Pole, see, 'cos it's a Polish ship, right? – he says, "Sorry, my darling," – they're so romantic, Poles – "sorry, but I must get you ashore." I say, "What, bad luck, is it, to have a woman on board?" And he says, "Bad luck for me when my wife sees you in Gdansk."

MRS Q. You're going to miss all this, Dolly.

DOLLY. I won't miss *it*. I'll miss them, the people, the comradeship. Yes, I'll miss that.

RED BARON. I always have done.

SPOT *(to* WHIPPET*)*. Hello, sonny. What's your name?

MRS Q. His name is Leonard, and his Mum's a friend of mine, all right?

CABBAGE *(to* WHIPPET*)*. There's one boss, we calls him Sweet Lips, he's always patient and understanding – in a word, drunk. Hoho, you know why we calls him Sweet Lips?

MRS Q. Stop that. I won't have indecent talk in here, you know my rules. Any more of it and you're out.

CABBAGE. It's only because –

MRS Q. Hey, never miss a good chance to shut up.

CABBAGE. Even on Dolly's last day –

MRS Q. Last day, Christmas Day, or Judgement Day – in here, rules is rules.

CABBAGE. Have you got a soft spot in you, Mrs Q?

MRS Q. Not that you'll ever touch.

MAGICOTE. Out of luck again, Cabbage Water.

MRS Q. Cabbage Water, Dolly Gray, Male Model, Crazy Horse … The names, all the names. It's like a party in here lunchtimes, them with all their names. And the porters from the vegetable market, and city gents, actors, sailors, the docks ratcatcher.

    CABBAGE *bites the head off a banana.*

RED BARON. Better make the most of it while you've still got it here.

MRS Q. What do you mean? It's always been here. If it wasn't, where would we be?

SONG. Is there a docker in the house
    Who'll tell us how it came to pass
    They stuck a port in a city up
    A river like an optic glass?
    Wasn't it obvious ships would come
    A cropper, wind up on their arse?
    Seven miles up a twisting gorge
    With a tide of fifty feet
    That sometimes overflows the quay
    And floods the houses on the street –
    What a place to build a port,

Just because two rivers meet.
Who had the bright idea?
What is it doing here?
Who had the bright idea?
What is it doing here?

HARRY. The Bristol Channel is the gateway
To the Western seas,
Trade from Europe, Africa,
America and the Indies.
Take a line through Lundy Isle, extend it
Far enough to westward, and you'll hit
The Nantucket Lightship at the harbour mouth
Of
New York, New York,
(It's a wonderful town) ...

SPOT. And Bristol Port
Will – be – shut – down.

DOCKERS. No! No! No!

HARRY. It's just the spot when there's
A fear we face a host
Of bloodthirsty corsairs
Swarming up from the Barbary Coast,
Scimitars in their teeth,
Villains from Ali Baba –
Then Bristol port's a fine and dandy harbour.
But now the threat is in
Containers from Bilbao.
Nice work if you can get it.
Won't you tell me how?

SONG. It is a city like a dream, a long street full of ships.
Beside the Quay a vessel mounting 80 guns may ride, but –
The slimy Avon at low water scarcely wets your hips.
Small wonder, then, that wiser men predict the port will shut!

ALL *(uproar)*. No! No!

SONG. Look at it east, west, north and south,
Up the Feeder, down the 'mouth –
Who had the bright idea?
What is it doing here?

SPOT. End your dream. That piddling stream

31

Is useless now, it's had its day.
The City Dock will get a shock.
They'll shut it down. It's close of play.
DOCKERS. But this is how we've earned our wage
Ever since the Middle Age.
SPOT. You've been asleep a thousand years.
Your eyes will open full of tears.
DOCKERS. The City Dock for centuries hence
Will still have work for every man.
SPOT. It can't go on. It makes no sense.
The City Dock is down the pan.
DOCKERS. No! No! No!
SONG. Look at it east, west, north and south,
Up the Feeder, down the 'Mouth.
Who had the bright idea?
What is it doing here?

It is a city like a dream, a long street full of ships.
Beside the Quay a vessel mounting 80 guns may ride, but –
The slimy Avon at low water scarcely wets your hips.
Small wonder, then, that wiser men predict the port will die!
[*Optional lines for band to chant as required:*
The Avon's just a pool of slush.
Bristol port's a busted flush.
On your bike you've got to go.
Find a job in Felixstowe.
Pack your bags, no time to spare.
It's not dark yet but it's getting there.]
Doors have opened. Train puffs by, hauling trucks.

INTERVAL

Doors closed. Pub.
SONG. Look at it east, west, north and south,
Up the Feeder, down the 'Mouth.
Who had the bright idea?
What is it doing here?

WHIPPET. What *is* it doing here?

MRS Q. I'll answer that. The true story of the Port of Bristol.

SONG. In Twelve forty AD
To everyone's surprise
The Bristol city fathers
Show some enterprise.

The Frome was just a rivulet,
To Bristol Bridge it led.
So they dig a half-mile trench
Down past W Shed.

RED BARON *as CABOT*. My name is Giovanni Caboto.
A new day, a new dollar's my motto.
They think I'm exploring.
Exploring? It's boring.
I'm out to make money, a lotto.

MRS Q. We know he won't find no Japan or China.

CABBAGE. We've been over there regular. It's the codfish, see.
Teeming, they are. You can pull 'em out in baskets. No one else
knows about it. Apart from the cod, forget it.

MRS Q. So we try to put him off it. But oh no, he doth have to go
and see for himself, he doth. And now they're all on to it.

CABBAGE. We should've knifed him, and had done with it.

SONG. By Seventeen hundred and nought
We've got a prosperous port.
From America vessels come
With sugar, tobacco and kegs of rum.

DOLLY. But the ships are always getting bigger, look.

MRS Q. At low water, they sit on mud.

HAPPY PAPPY *as SCOUSE*. In Liverpool, we've got two *wet* docks, like.

SONG. In Seventeen thirty-five
A committee speaks as one:
If you want this port to thrive
Something has to be done.

MAGICOTE *as MAYOR*. Too expensive.

SONG. Trinkets, guns and gin
Were sent out on the waves,
And when they got to Africa
They traded them for slaves.

33

DOLLY *as PINNEY*. Surely God ordained them for the use and benefit of us, otherwise his divine will would have been made manifest by some sign.

GOD. Hands off those Africans, Bristol!

DOLLY *as PINNEY*. But it's duty free. He's overlooked that.

SONG. In Seventeen eighty-seven
    Seeing how things were run
    A floating Harbour is proposed –
    Something has to be done.

MAGICOTE *as MAYOR*. Something has to be done. So what we'll do is, we'll appoint a committee.

MRS Q The committee recommends that something has to be done.

MAGICOTE *as MAYOR*. Too expensive.

SONG. By eighteen hundred and ten
    The floating Harbour's a fact.
    But it cost twice the estimate.
    How do we get our money back?

MAGICOTE *as MAYOR*. We'll raise the charges!

DOLLY. So a trader paying £22 a year at Gloucester gets told in Bristol –

MAGICOTE *as MAYOR*. That'll be £614 please.

CABBAGE. This port is failing because of our town dues and mayor's dues and heavy local taxation.

MAGICOTE *as MAYOR*. We'll thank you to keep your hasty opinions to yourself.

MRS Q. A quarter of the civic income goes on banquets.

MAGICOTE *as MAYOR*. What is this, the inquisition?

SONG. It isn't only water
    The harbour's holding in.
    It's sewage too. The stink
    Would make a docker blink.

MAGICOTE *as MAYOR*. We'll build a culvert to take it down the New Cut.

WHIPPET. Now Bedminster gets the stench instead.

MAGICOTE *as MAYOR*. Only till next century, see.

SONG. In Eighteen thirty-seven
    You've not seen nothing finer –
    Isambard Kingdom Brunel builds
    The first Atlantic liner.

HAPPY PAPPY. But the port can't handle it.

CABBAGE *as BRUNEL.* What's required is a pier at Portishead, a dock at Sea Mills, and a wider entrance to the floating harbour.

MAGICOTE *as MAYOR.* Too expensive. *(Snatches cigar from BRUNEL's mouth)* And you're setting a bad example.

CABBAGE *as BRUNEL.* So my Great Western has to go on anchoring off the mouth of the Avon, and transferring passengers and cargo in boats?

MAGICOTE *as MAYOR.* Right. And that'll be £200 a time. Just 'cos your ship's too big for our dock don't mean you can get away without paying us nothing.

HAPPY PAPPY. His response is to build a ship three times bigger, the Great Britain.

SONG. In Eighteen forty-three
    It steamed out on the main,
    Returned a century later
    On a zimmer frame.

MRS Q. The Great Britain is a disaster for Bristol. We can't cope with the ships getting bigger.

HAPPY PAPPY. Half a lifetime after Brunel proposed it, a dock is built at Avonmouth – and a rival dock at Portishead.

DOLLY. You waits 35 years for a dock, then two come along at once.

RED BARON. Avonmouth, now that was the place to grow up. A pulsulating, live place. The hum and clang of the grain elevators, cranes whining, winches rattling, capstans heaving, shunters puffing, the shouting and bawling, the blast of a ship's whistle and the acknowledging toot from a tug. Nowadays, they've got gates. You can't wander about. If you could take the wife and kids for a stroll around the dock, show them what you're doing and what boats are in there, like that you used to see the beauty of it.

MRS Q. When the grain comes in, the whole of Avonmouth has a wonderful mealy smell.

RED BARON. You assume everyone where you live is a docker, apart from the policeman and the teacher. One or two work for ICI, but they're like aliens.

MRS Q. Things come in loose, and are spilled, and so you get foreign plants growing, beautiful moths and butterflies, that have come in on plantlife and hatched. They're not British moths. It's an exotic place, Avonmouth is.

SPOT. Me, I wouldn't want to have grown up anywhere except round here. People with a clerical-type job, they don't venture into the streets around the wharves. Yet it's the heart of the city.

HAPPY PAPPY. When we were children we used to stay outside our house in Prince Street until 10 o'clock at night. We see all the merchant seamen going up the Centre to have a few drinks. They never spoke a wrong word to us at all. German, Danish, Norwegian, Dutch …

MRS Q. The Greeks. They're lovely fellows.

CABBAGE. Poles. I heard this Pole ordering a coffee. "I'll have it without cream. If you haven't got any cream, I'll have it without milk."

HAPPY PAPPY. The dock labourers raised their hats to our mother, or any woman.

DOLLY. Good evening, madam.

HAPPY PAPPY. My mother told me, in Queen Square years ago they had sheep grazing. The dockers, when they didn't have any work on, they'd go and sit on the benches and talk, and look at the sheep.

SONG. King Billy's mounted in Queen Square,
　　　Admire his flowing locks.
　　　His face towards the Customs House,
　　　His arse towards the docks.

HAPPY PAPPY. They turned the statue around after that.

SONG. The King, the Mayor, the Corporation,
　　　Money's all their passion.
　　　That's what they mean when they want things
　　　Shipshape and Bristol fashion.

SPOT. The river police have a hut over there by the bridge. Two bells means there's somebody in the river, the police take a boat out, and if we hear it, like uncles and that, they go down. Our grandfather once, in dense fog, and ice on the water, he held up a struggling woman for an hour before anyone heard his shouts. She was taken to the Infirmary, and soon after became a mother. She asked for our Grandad to visit her, and when he got there she cursed him.

WHIPPET. She was in that much trouble?

SPOT. We do get that around here.

HAPPY PAPPY. The country bus station was right by us. A bus goes up to the Co-op to turn around. It's so foggy the driver tells the conductor, "Get out and see where I am." The conductor goes down the steps, right in the dock, and drowns.

SPOT. We had a cousin always wore plus fours. Down the docks, he falls right in, and his feet come up first. His feet come up first and he comes up afterwards!

HAPPY PAPPY. There were three bombs dropped in Prince Street. The last one, this fireman said every time he tried to get at it, so it went further into the mud. It's still there. So be careful when you go down Prince Street. Run, don't walk! Don't wear hobnail boots.

DOLLY. You grow up in Hotwells or Cliftonwood, you walk along past Albion Dockyard – always two big ships building on the stocks.

MRS Q. When they launch the boats, they're on thick chains. You see all the men that's worked on them, down the side, watching. And then you hear the clanking of all the chains. The brass band's playing. Me and my sisters get up there and go 'heave ho, heave ho'. One ship, they nearly lost. He came down too fast, right across the river and hit the Mardyke wall.

DOLLY. That was the last City boat. Chicago City.

MRS Q. You never had more than two dresses, one in the wash, one you're wearing.

[Underlining: SPOT as MOTHER or FATHER.]

SPOT. My poor mother. We used to go home filthy. When things wore out, there's ways. We were forever asking – When's tea, Mum? When your Dad gets in. What we having? Wait and see, like I has to. Then, one day – Mum, Dad's coming up the road. There's something wrong with him. He can't walk proper. She goes and looks out the window. Oh my god, what's he been and done? He's put on stones of weight! And our Dad comes in the house sweating, with his coat like this *(huge)*. And he starts bringing out all these tins. Ye Olde Oake Ham. Stewed steak, from Ireland that is. Salmon. What you want for tea, then? Here's more Ye Olde Oake Ham. We had it with chips, beans, spaghetti, mashed potatoes, in sandwiches. When our Mum had to buy some, she was always loyal to Ye Olde Oake Ham. Then she says to us, <u>Now grab hold of that</u>. And we take hold of this length of curtain he's got wrapped round him, and he turns and turns until he's got it all off himself. He tells us, <u>New curtains for the front of the house there, look nice</u>. And our Mum chimes in, <u>And dresses for the girls</u>. Then he says, <u>Oh, I forgot. Cockle boat's in</u>. He removes these plastic bags he's got over his trousers, and they're full of cockles. Then he tells us to make ourselves scarce, and when he thinks we're out the way, only actually we're peeping through the crack of the door, he tells her, <u>And here's summat for you, Maggie</u>. And he starts peeling off all these pairs of long knickers he's got on, all different colours – pink, green, peach … About six pair he'd got on him. He says, <u>Passion killers. Silk, they are. Lovely</u>. And our Mum, we can see she's trying to keep a straight face, and she says, <u>I'll get 'em washed straight away and put 'em all side by side on the line to drive that Alice Gerrish next door mad</u>. Oh yes, there's ways all right.

MRS Q. When our Dad was at Avonmouth, you'd come home and find the house was suddenly full of huge blocks of New Zealand cheddar. Or matches. Pencils. Daps. When he died – people say funny things, don't they – a friend told me, "It's lucky he went when he did. He could've gone inside."

CABBAGE. Our brother, he did go to prison, for his beliefs.

MRS Q. What are they?

CABBAGE. He believed he could run faster than the coppers.

RED BARON. Look at it this way, Mrs Q. The dockers are ill paid by firms who are making enormous profits. My kids are mostly dressed in jumble-sale stuff.

MRS Q. That's all very well. But they Guinness barrels from Dublin, if a leaker's found it's put aside and encouraged to leak faster, into the mugs they take down with them. One gang of rascals takes a set of tools to make sure they find leakers. And stop them up again. So by the time they get to me they're two gallons short measure. Why I don't spend my evenings tucked up with a nice hot-water bottle between me I'll never know.

SPOT. Where we lived before, St Philips, The Dings, Phillyifi Street, Milk Street – hovels it was, tenements. One communal tap in the middle of the yard.

CABBAGE. Crew's Hole, the stench of it – glue, manure, knackers, bonemeal, tar, creosote, that's what we had there.

SPOT. So what happens? We're all moved out, under a grand new scheme, this estate at Knowle West, right? Then they just forget us. They give us one pub – one pub and all of us up there. And there's families who've been fighting from day one put next door to each other. That is the psychology of the Bristol Council.

MAGICOTE. Do you wonder men do the pierhead jump?

WHIPPET. Why? Have you done it?

MAGICOTE. I've done it. I run foul of a German woodwork master. I'm making a stand for my pet parrot, and I don't do anything right for this gentleman. He has a piece of wood and he keeps smacking my hand. By the blackboard, he has his watch hung up there. I've got a wooden mallet in my hand and I shout out, "You German bastard" and I throw the mallet. Well, I miss his head and I hit his watch, and the watch goes in pieces. Course I know then, I'm bang in trouble, so I push off home, along St John's Lane. There's no one home. What am I going to do? I wander over Victoria Park, down through St Luke's Road, over the bridge, up into Cathay. Alongside Redcliffe Church, have a look at the pet shop, cross the road and down into Guinea Street, there. And I'm looking at the boats unloading and thinking, what am I going to do now? But being at the docks takes my mind off my problems. I'm watching this peculiar craft, and some unusual looking men, in my eyes, 'cos you know, I'm 13, I've never seen Norwegian or Greeks or Danish. Big blond blokes, dark swarthy people. This is outside the Ostrich Inn. They're up from Avonmouth for stores and they're drinking. A funny smell comes in. Cor, what's that smell?

OLAF *(on gantry)*. Whales, me boy.

MAGICOTE. I don't know what a whale is.

OLAF. We're on our way. Are you looking for a job?

MAGICOTE. Yeah.

OLAF. We could do with a ship's boy.

MAGICOTE. I don't know what a ship's boy is. But here's a chance to get away.

OLAF. Go and get some clothes. Arrange it with your mother and father so everything's okay, and you'll get your ship's note and the captain will post it off to them. All right?

MAGICOTE. I run home all the way. Gets in, pack a couple of pair of socks, couple of pair of trousers, me daps, me overcoat which I have, and that's me lot. I never had much clothes. We aren't rich or nothing. I leave a note to me mother saying, you know, I'm joining a ship. Don't know what the hell I'm doing. I gets on board this – I know what it is now, a chaser. Size of a tug, but the harpoon gun in front. Down Cheddar Gorge, through Prince Street gate, Hotwells, to the Cumberland Basin. Waiting for the tide, so they can open the gate. Under the Suspension Bridge, looking up at the Avon Gorge rocks. I've never seen them like that – it's magnificent. Will I ever see it again? That is in my thoughts. Get down to Avonmouth, in the main dock and alongside this – it is some ship, 19- or 20-thousand tonner. Go on board her and the first mate takes me down to sign the articles. I don't know what articles is.

OLAF *(mumbles).* Joining on of your own free will … Have permission from your mother and father …

MAGICOTE. All that rubbish. They just want a crew member. They don't care if a trained monkey had come aboard, they'd take that. My job is galley boy. I'm away two years. Hunting the whales into Iceland. Back up into the Western Ocean. Unload oil at Halifax, Nova Scotia, and take on stores. Then follow the whales right the way down south, Tristan Da Cunha, and to the Cape. You fish there. Unload oil at the Falkland Islands, get on stores. Then fish across off Cape Town, Durban. The whales was migrating into the Pacific then. Follow them into the Indian Ocean, then the Malacca Straits. And I spend my fifteenth birthday in Kobe, in Japan.

SONG. Otanjoubi omedetou, otanjoubi omedetou,
      Otanjoubi omedetou Magicote-san, otanjoubi omedetou.

MAGICOTE. When you go ashore anywhere, everyone knows who you are. You stink. Cape Town, Durban, wild places. All the whores are around the docks. I'm not allowed in any bars, but I get in just the same. We've got over 300 crew on board, and 20 chasing vessels all with 15, 20 men on them. And we're not the only factory ship there, you have Japanese, American, German, the whole convoy. It's a magnificent sight, mind. Everyone fighting to catch the whales. And when they get ashore and get the booze in them … Their skinning knives are about that long, like a little broadsword. And there's blokes getting stabbed and slashed. When I get back, after two years, they're glad to see me again. My father gives me a damn good hiding. But I've seen it all. Like, been around the world. At 15, seeing all these things. And getting paid.

WHIPPET *(sings)*. Far away places,
    With magnetic names,
    Caracas, Odessa,
    Macao, Conakry,
    There's a place for you and me ...
    Worse things happen at sea ...

    No place like home. You come ashore,
    But it's no place to be once more.
    It's worse than before, you're down with a bump,
    So what do you do? The pierhead jump.

CABBAGE. The years when I was at sea, Mum and Dad moved house about three times. But I found them every time.

DOLLY. I've heard say that a deep water man wets himself when he sights land. Whereas your coasting man, your rock dodger, he wets himself when he loses sight of land.

CABBAGE. I should know. I done both.

HAPPY PAPPY. So you wets yourself everywhere.

HARRY. You want to talk about seafaring ...

CABBAGE. When I came off the last ship, I stood on the quay and I said, "Farewell. The next time I go to sea I'll be a passenger." But I never done it.

HAPPY PAPPY. Pie in the sky.

MAGICOTE. Castles in the air.

RED BARON *(drinking up)*. I've heard enough metaphors for one day.

MRS Q. Hey, watch your mouth, right?

RED BARON. Eh?

MRS Q. I heard you.

HAPPY PAPPY. Mrs Q, you ever been seized by an urge to let your hair down, throw off your clacks and dance a wild, abandoned dance of savage joy?

MRS Q. No.

HAPPY PAPPY. Only asking.

HARRY. Real seafaring now ...

CABBAGE. We're back to work.

    GANG *exit. Doors open. During* SONG, GANG *are loading.*

HARRY. If you grew up, as I did, in Pill, you were conversant with boats from boyhood. All the pilots came from Pill. They had it sewn up. In the old days, they'd row out as far as Lundy, seeking an incoming ship, and racing each other to get to her first. My family were pilots. But I started on the tugs.

SONG. Oh I remember Barry Roads when I was a tugboat boy,
　　　　The bustle and the hooting and the swearing and the joy;
　　　　Tramps and steamers laden with fine Welsh anthracite
　　　　Bound out across the ocean to keep the world alight.

　　　　The laughter and the music from the passing paddle-steamers
　　　　(That's what they think the sea's about, these two-bob day-
　　　　　　　　　　　　　　　　　　　　　　　　trip dreamers);
　　　　An Osborne & Wallis coaster off to Portishead;
　　　　The Queen Mother pilot cutter, foam white and regal red.

　　　　So we zigzagged to our station (which was all we ever did)
　　　　As out from Barry Docks the Sharpness pilot slid ...
　　　　Oh of all the summer evenings that I've stored in memory's
　　　　　　　　　　　　　　　　　　　　　　　　chest
　　　　Those boyhood ones in Barry are the ones I treasure best.
　　　　We came up slowly through the roads to stem against the
　　　　　　　　　　　　　　　　　　　　　　　　tide,
　　　　When she stole like a dream upon us with a cool majestic
　　　　　　　　　　　　　　　　　　　　　　　　pride –
　　　　The old four-master Viking, deep with Australian grain.
　　　　And we gaped at her and marvelled as we never would again.

　　　Loading continues.

CABBAGE. You looking to make a few bob, lad?

WHIPPET. What is it?

CABBAGE. I need a hand this evening. Moving heavy plant.

WHIPPET. What, a tree, like?

CABBAGE. Like machinery. I needs you out in the van with me, out Pilning way. Got some machinery to deliver.

WHIPPET. I don't know.

CABBAGE. Five bob in it for you. Just take an hour.

WHIPPET. What kind of machinery?

CABBAGE. It don't matter what kind of machinery. It's plant that's surplus to requirements where it is.

WHIPPET. Where is it?

CABBAGE. In my front room, behind the armchair.

WHIPPET. Why me?

CABBAGE. It's a simple job, so I need someone simple. You do the talking if we gets stopped. You found it in the road and thought you'd better get it back to the dock.

HAPPY PAPPY. Over the beam!

DOLLY. It's a cat and mouse game, non-stop. This copper told me, he sees a docker leaving at the end of the day, he's looking peeky. *(As COPPER)* You all right?

HAPPY PAPPY. Yeh.

DOLLY *as COPPER*. But there's something about him. You'd better come inside. *(HAPPY PAPPY sits down.)* If you're going to give them the rub-down, you take them inside. Everyone's got their dignity. He's sitting there and he's looking really ill. And I see a pool of water round his shoes. You pissed yourself?

HAPPY PAPPY. What, frightened of you?

DOLLY *as COPPER*. And then he keels over. And he's reaching down, and it turns out he's got all these frozen lamb's kidneys in his underpants. I hadn't found them because, well, you don't shove your hand down a bloke's goolies first off. I'm cautioning you under the Larceny Act. Can you account for your possession of these kidneys?

HAPPY PAPPY. Sod the kidneys, you prat. What about me knackers?

DOLLY. He had to go to hospital. After that, they called him Conker Bollocks.

RED BARON. The docker is the biggest thief in the country. They're like seagulls.

CABBAGE. There was a kid tealeafed a brand new set of wheels for his Mini. When they went round to arrest him he'd got 84 batteries there as well.

HAPPY PAPPY. You see one man do it, you almost feel it's expected of you. And when it comes to the Pen Manager hisself tells you to get his car loaded up with potatoes, well ...

DOLLY. This bloke nicks enough best Finland tongued and grooved to make hisself two pigeon houses. I says to him, I don't know what I'm doing here tallying, when you're pinching half of it. Only he ties some of it under his car with plastic string, and the exhaust burns through it, so when the copper stops him at the gate it all hits the deck.

CABBAGE *(mimes car)*. What joker put that under there, then?

HAPPY PAPPY. Over the beam!

  MAGICOTE *climbing out of hold with bulging coat.* GANG *sing the Dick Barton tune, while* DOLLY *as* COPPER *walks suspiciously past.*

DOLLY *as* COPPER. What you got under there?

MAGICOTE *(Bristol moan)*. I'm expecting.

DOLLY *as* COPPER. You're what?

MAGICOTE. I'm expecting that you'll look the other way now, and later you'll find some of it in the rowers' hut for you.

RED BARON. There's this bloke pinches a whole box of boots. Opens it up, flipping heck, they're all left boots. So he goes through the hold opening up every box looking for right boots. What he don't know is that the shippers are wise to blokes like him, and they send all the right boots on a different boat.

DOLLY. They like Triumph Heralds, on the dock. Under that bonnet, it's just the right space for a whole lamb.

HAPPY PAPPY. There was a PC flat on the seats searching the glove compartment, and this bloke sits down on him and drives away, up the motorway.

CABBAGE. And another one, he thinks he sees something on the back seat, so he dives in through the open top, and they go off with his feet sticking up through the roof.

HAPPY PAPPY. It must be something in the Bristol water. The tugboat crews, they moor up next to a ship with better ropes, next morning the ropes have been changed over and they're away. You know what they say in Wales? What the Bristol men can't carry, they'll roll. That coal stack over by Barry, we're helping ourselves, to keep the home fires burning. This gaffer has his suspicions, so he whitewashes over the top of the stack. Well, we move the white bits out the way, take what we need, and put the white ones back on top.

CABBAGE *as* TAFF. That whitewash, it's shrinking the coal.

MAGICOTE. They shanghaied some Avonmouth blokes up here one day, and they weren't used to our standard of living. They got all boozed up, and we had to fetch 'em out of the hold with a crane.

  RED BARON *is unloading pallets.* GANG *watch.*

DOLLY. It's gone eight o'clock, which is a very ticklish time for dockers. It works like this, see. If your ship finishes before 12 noon you're only on the half a day, so it's find another job, or go home. Finish after 12 noon, you can go home when it's done and you still gets your pay for the whole day. Now it's the same with overtime. You have a half an hour allowance for tea, then half past five to half past eight, this is overtime. But if you work on after that you get paid for all night, and you have a day off next day. If you're working and the job's finishing, he'll come along and call out, "You work to a finish tonight." And you're looking at the clock and if it's gone eight –

SONG. Make it last a little longer,
That's the ticket on the dock.
Take it easy, you'll be stronger.
Keep your eye upon the clock.

When an accident is needed,
You arrange a little knock – oh,
Our work has been impeded!
Keep your eye upon the clock.

DOLLY. What you reckon, then?

HAPPY PAPPY. He's not happy. There's only one pallet to go, look.

DOLLY *(glance at clock)*. Four minutes to half past eight. He'll work the oracle.

CABBAGE. Four minutes. There's men can run a mile in four minutes.

MAGICOTE. Old Red, all he'd run a mile for is to avoid heavy work.

DOLLY. He'll come up trumps. He's creative, is Red. He can do less in four minutes than you can do in an hour.

HAPPY PAPPY. Eh?

DOLLY. You knows what I mean.

HAPPY PAPPY. The pallet's going. He is not a happy docker.

DOLLY. Watch.

RED BARON *drops pallet. Contents tumble out. He feigns dismay.*

WHIPPET. What a pro. He could idle for England, him.

DOLLY. He is sly and devious, and I mean that in the very best sense of those words.

MAGICOTE. There should be a hall of fame for dockers like Red.

CABBAGE. There is. They calls it the Labour Exchange.

GANG *make a production of clearing up.*

SONG. When an accident is needed,
You arrange a little knock – oh,

45

Our work has been impeded!

Keep your eye upon the clock.

CABBAGE. See the way some food's handled, you'd never eat it.

SONG. The trick is in the timing.

Hear the tick, hear the tock –

Nine will soon be chiming.

Keep your eye upon the clock.

CABBAGE *is hiding oranges down inside each trouser leg. He looks up at the audience. Gesture – palm back, whistle.*

CABBAGE. I've had legs down here. Legs of lamb.

Work is finished. Hooter sounds.

STEVEDORE. There 'tis, then. Get your books and go home.

SONG. Half past eight. We blew it.

Should have stopped and taken stock.

It's the only way to do it,

Keep your eye upon the clock.

CABBAGE *gives* HAPPY PAPPY *a couple of his oranges.* DEREK *and* KIT *run up to meet* DOLLY.

DEREK. What you got for us tonight?

KIT. Oranges!

DOLLY. I don't want to see you eating the rind on them oranges, mind. They come all the way from Africa, and there's no toilets on the boats, so when the seamen's up there and they wants to have a quick pee – that's why you gets that stinging round your mouth. Remember that any time they throw you one from the boat.

KIDS *exit. Everyone else heads for pub.* HARRY *is up on his bridge. Doors closing.*

HARRY. You're a bit on edge watching them onload, because you've got to catch the tide. You can't risk leaving late, not in Bristol Docks. There's not much margin. But once you're at sea, the coastal trade is easygoing. You don't plough through the weather like the Queen Mary. You go into shelter, if you're caught in a Sou'west gale. As first mate you're the dogsbody of the ship. You do everything. You're thin, athletic, you're all about. Soon as you become skipper, you let everybody else do the work and just keep your eye on it. And you usually grow rather fat, and relax. *(Fog music.)* Until something happens. We had loaded pig-iron in

46

Holland. All being well, I'll be home for the weekend with Jeanne, in Abbot's Leigh.

SONG. He's an old sea dog ... dog ... dog ... dog ...

HARRY. We drop the pilot. Fog is setting in.
Find our way across the grey North Sea
From buoy to buoy, until the middle watch,
The black of night. And then out go our lights.

MAGICOTE *(calls)*. The generator's packed up. I'm working on it.

HARRY. The radar's down, we have gone way off course.
(Calls) Drop the anchor!
We sit upon the sea like men gone blind.
Water lapping is the only sound.

CABBAGE *(calls)*. I think I hear the whistle on the West Hinder Buoy.

HARRY. Chief?

MAGICOTE *(calls)*. Still working on the bugger.

HARRY. Light the oil lantern by the binnacle.
We'll do it by the compass and our ears.
So past the Goodwin Sands and down the Channel,
Chugging through a white world 20 yards
Across before it ends in walls of fog.

SONG. Fog ... Fog ... Fog ... Fog ...

HARRY. Sometimes we stop and listen through the fog
For diaphone, whistle, reed, explosive charge,
Signals like fallen stars from the unseen sky.
St Catherine's, the Shambles Lightship, Portland Bill
Past the Race. Each time we blow our whistle
No answer comes. We are alone at sea.

CABBAGE. You must drop anchor, sir. We'll have a collision. Or you'll run us aground.

HARRY. I carry on. I won't give in, not now.

SONG. Fog ... Fog ... Fog ... Fog ...

HARRY. The Start, Lizard, Wolf, Longships, Pendeen
Go by unseen but heard. A hundred miles
To go now, to get home. We're listening out
For Trevose Head and Hartland Point. No sound.
Nor Lundy South Light. The Bristol Channel tide
Drives us from the straight course. So I stop
And drift between the Scarweather Sands and the Gower.

Both coasts have given sailors savage welcome.
And then our ship's radio touches hands
With the Juno, homeward bound from Dublin.
They see us as a radar blip, and give
Us a bearing. My reckoning's three miles out.

SONG. He's an old sea dog … dog … dog … dog …

HARRY. As we dock all hell breaks loose. By the time I get home to Abbot's Leigh it's blowing a hurricane. It sinks the ferry Princess Victoria in the Irish Sea, with many lives lost, and raises a tide right over the Dutch dykes. On our next trip over there, in the sea we go past a milking byre with the carcass of a cow still chained to it.

CABBAGE. And he was screaming, "It's taken my finger off! It's taken my finger off!" And Joe tells him, "Spit on it and stick it back on."

HAPPY PAPPY. Any accident on the dock's going to be a serious one. But they are a callous lot, dockers.

MAGICOTE. A sling of aluminium comes down and breaks a chap's toes. But it's a Sunday, and they're going like the clappers to earn double-time money, so they just pick him up and park him in the 'tween decks and leave him there till the lunch break while they go on working. He's sitting there in the corner for an hour in agony.

HAPPY PAPPY. You should see us swagging grain up the dancers. It's a circus turn. You run with a two-hundredweight sack from the hold across the open hatch on two narrow shivers and run back again for more. When you get home, your wife has to soak the shirt off your back.

DOLLY. I fell off a stack and all I know is my ankle went click, click. I never lost no time. I just hobbled around over it. But when I go for the medical. *(As DOCTOR)* I'm afraid that in about four years from now you'll be in a wheelchair, Mr Gray. You won't be able to work. *(As himself)* It's what they call chronic peronial thickening of the ankle. Whatever that is. About a year after I did it, I caught it again, between two iron skips, where I had a lump. And that must have pushed it back into place again. Apart from a bit of an ache, now and again, I haven't had no trouble with it at all. It's right as rain.

HAPPY PAPPY. I've always wondered what is so right about rain.

DOLLY. Still do wonder. Two drops and it's close down the hatches, only half a day's pay today, go on, go home.

CABBAGE. There's more killed docking than in the mines.

MAGICOTE. Asbestos, I've handled thousands of bags of that. We played snowballs with it.

HAPPY PAPPY. Grain dust, it's so thick sometimes you can't see men. A grain gang I was in, the other five all died by their early 40s.

DOLLY. We've had chaps died by lambs coming out and hits them on the head. Frozen lamb.

MAGICOTE. Those three on the concentrate, remember? They'd been skimming off a bit of cheap, but at the back of the stack, by the engine room, it had dried out, and it comes down and buries them. One got out, but the other two didn't.

DOLLY. There's no Social Security, so every Thursday, when you get your pay, you have a table outside for nobbins. The blokes throw 10 shillings or five shillings or whatever they can afford on it. That's the only kind of help a docker gets. Apart from a very small insurance benefit. The first day's work we do, they stop one and ninepence. And a penny for, I don't know what the penny is for. I've never wondered what the penny is for.

HAPPY PAPPY. When a man's too old to do it, it's no good him standing there. He's got to find a job that's easier.

CABBAGE. Yeah, and less money.

MAGICOTE. Tally clerk is for people that are injured, or as you got older and don't feel up to it. Or you end up with a brush and wheelbarrow.

DOLLY. We had a chap, 90 years old he was. He'd go round trucking, tea and things. Joe Pring. And when it slacked off a bit, he'd walk home. He'd walk home from Avonmouth to Kingsdown. Seven miles, would that be? Eight? Eventually, they made him stop, and he was dead within the week.

MAGICOTE. There was that weekend conference on welfare. Could we find out whose responsibility it is to put a toilet roll in the lavatories? No. The Dock Labour Board say –

HAPPY PAPPY. "We're very sorry, it's not our pigeon."

MAGICOTE. The Port of Bristol Authority say –

HAPPY PAPPY. "Sorry, no, not down to us."

MAGICOTE. The stevedores we work for –

CABBAGE. "Well, you might not be working for us tomorrow."

MAGICOTE. Now, with this talk of decasualisation, you hear the bosses squeal –

HAPPY PAPPY. "Why should we pay them when there's no work for them?" It's pure chicanery.

MAGICOTE. And so it goes on.

HAPPY PAPPY. What *is* chicanery?

CABBAGE. We did get a canteen. It took a world war. Most of us still go in the pub.

DOLLY *(to* RED BARON*).* Have a farewell drink with me?

RED BARON. It's not *my* last day, is it?

HAPPY PAPPY. It would be if some of they bosses had their way.

RED BARON. They won't be having their way while I'm still around. I wonder why it is they all take an instant dislike to me?

HAPPY PAPPY. It saves time.

RED BARON. If they'd stop telling lies about us, I'd stop telling the truth about them. Them and the Union. Both our enemies.

WHIPPET. The Union, our enemy?

RED BARON. The Union is never for the working man. It's always, "All in order." It's "all in order, all in order", all the bloody time. No matter what complaint you go out with, it's "All in order."

DOLLY. They just don't want to cause any argument. All they want is to sit in the Union office and drink their cups of tea. Most of them are people who, when they were workers, used to stir up the most trouble. They go in a Union office and turn over the other way.

RED BARON. If a certain type of docker goes for a Union official's job, nobody says it openly, but the heads are nodding. "Yeah, he'll do, he'll do for us."

WHIPPET. I don't know why you bother to have a trade union then.

MAGICOTE. Because without a union we are sitting ducks, to be picked off one by one, by the employers. In a union, at least we are a flock of ducks. They can't shoot us all. Not all at once, any rate.

[Underlining: STEVEDORE *voice, then* UNION OFFICIAL *voice.]*

RED BARON. You rely on the Union, you're up a ladder with no rungs. Me, I'm a militant and proud of it. If there's a smell under the sink, get rid of it. I've become radio-active. I won't let go. This

is how the aluminium strike started. To push those hoists in a barge requires the full strength of every six-man down there. The stevedore takes out two, and leaves us with four, saying – Nothing to do with me. They give you extra money.
CABBAGE. What extra money?
RED BARON. Five-eighths of a penny a ton. You're joking. Well, you must take that up with your Union official. But he ain't out of bloody bed yet. (This is eight o'clock in the morning) Right, we'll give it a miss. You can't, Can't we? Thee bist all a load of bloody loonies.

Up the ladder we go, to the Union office, wait an hour, then down the road comes this all-done-up-like-a-dog's-dinner Union official. He always looked tidy because he never did anything. What's this game, then? It was signed last week. You never let us know.

Well, you haven't had an aluminium boat in till now. We had to find out the hard way, did we? I tell you what, we ain't working four men in the barge, we're working six men. What about the increase? You can stick it up your gunga. We'll work the old rate. But I've negotiated a new rate. And you took away two men. It was what the Port employer asked for. Well you go back and tell them Port employers to get stuffed. The man is a wretch. So, we go out and into the café down there, the Blackbird. We meet a lot of dockers. Right, brothers, this is what's happening. Now, are you with us?
ALL. Sure we're with you.
RED BARON. And the whole docks comes to a stop. Costs the town two million quid, the stoppage. One month. We never got the men back. And I never got a job on the aluminium again. (Shaking head) The Union's collusion with the Port of Bristol employers always did stink to high heaven.
HAPPY PAPPY. You're wasted here, Red. You ought to be up The Downs Sunday evenings.
DOLLY. Comrades, let us assume, just for a moment, that the Prime Minister is not lying …
    Honking car interrupts him.
And when the revolution comes we will all be driving Daimlers.
MAGICOTE. I don't want a Daimler.

DOLLY. You will drive what you're bloody well told to drive.

HAPPY PAPPY. I'll tell you how wonderful the Port of Bristol Authority is. They've built this brand new crane, right? But then they find it's too short, it only reaches halfway across the ships you get now. So we has to unload one side of the ship, and then wait while it turns round, to do the other side.

CABBAGE. Hold on, brother. What's this you've got in your pocket?

WHIPPET. I just found it lying around.

CABBAGE. A jar of Nesquick! Young Whippet has nicked a jar of Nesquick. Whippet Quick, that's your name. You're Whippet Quick, you are.

MRS Q *rings a bell.*

MRS Q. Drink up. It's nearly closing time.

MAGICOTE. We come to the last day of the ship, we're worried about whether we'll work tomorrow, rather than the satisfaction of the job well done. If someone came along and said – *(as STEVEDORE)* "We want to catch the six o'clock tide, we need your co-operation." Then us seeing the tugs put on that ship at half past five and pulling off the quay wall at 20 to six, we would have pride of workmanship. Instead – *(as STEVEDORE)* "Get your fingers out!" – the boss is trying to drive the job out by five o'clock. No knowledge at all must escape from the office down to the docker. Because if he knows anything he'll take advantage of it.

RED BARON. The dockers in the old days, they were militant. There was a strike over wages. Just before Christmas they march through Queen Square. The army's called in, they charge, eight dockers end up in hospital. And what does the local paper have to say about it? *(As EDITOR)* "The main result has been to spoil retail trade on what should have been one of the busiest nights of the year. The demonstration may have been fun for the unemployed, but it meant a serious blow to the shopkeepers."

HAPPY PAPPY. After the First War, they opposed the blockade of the Soviet Union. They blacked ships taking munitions to the British army in Ireland. They had a new leader, Ernie Bevin. The man who invented the Transport & General Workers Union.

CABBAGE. And went on to invent the self-puncturing bicycle tyre, which would be a whole lot more use to us.

DOLLY. A door-to-door soft drink salesman he was when he started down here. And he winds up Foreign Secretary.

CABBAGE. Fizzy lemonade, madam? Or could I interest you in my policy on the Soviet Union?

MRS Q. Closing time.

RED BARON. I go out there and there is a whole industry. And it is feudal. I'm fighting side by side with men who want to improve the conditions for everybody. The rates in Bristol are abominable. And it is done in collusion with the Union. Who go along to the meeting and say, 'Five-eighths of a penny a ton? Oh, we'll take it." Result? Strike. I could be a revolutionary leader. I've got the quality of it, there, to fire people up. But I can't get nobody to fire! That skiving docker who got himself on the City Council, he calls me a chameleon. Just because I voted Conservative once. Me! Just the once. I voted for Delphine Pullen. I fancied her. She comes calling on me as Conservative candidate for local municipal. I know her. She lives across the road there, Delphine. I have an eye for a lovely woman. And I vote for her. She gets in. He 'phones up. "You bloody chameleon." A chameleon turns colour. I haven't turned colour. "Whaa?"

RED BARON. I'm proud to be called a chameleon. By a reptile fucking expert.

MRS Q. Language! Up to now you've been very good. Don't go and spoil it or you'll be out for good, all of you. Come on, it's gone closing time.

Doors open. The ship is leaving.

MATE. You can't leave yet, sir. There are women aboard.

HARRY. We've got to leave, or we'll miss the tide.

MATE. But I can't find them. They've been stowed away.

SPOT *comes down gangway. As she leaves she blows a kiss to* COPPER.

With hooter blasts, rattle of chains, &c the ship leaves, HARRY *at helm.*

SONG. She's under way ...

She's under way ...

Our ship's under way ...

We hear the chains, we feel the screw's rotation,

The screaming gulls escort her out to sea.

She plots her course, she's got a destination.

We just make the best of destiny.

She's steaming off to ports in foreign waters,

Steaming off, and leaves us in her wake.

Tomorrow we must feed our sons and daughters,
Tomorrow there's another wage to make.

Another job if we can find it,
Another screw for pay,
Another ship behind it,
Another day.

The dock is a vacancy. Doors close.

MRS Q. It's closing time.

SONG. Can it last a little longer?
Hear the ticking of the clock.

MRS Q. It's closing time.

SONG. The hints are getting stronger.
Will they close the dock?

HAPPY PAPPY. There's talk, whispers in the paper. The trade is dying out in the City Docks, gradually. And the environmental lot would like to see the traffic out of the centre.

DOLLY. No one takes a blind bit of notice. Especially not the younger ones, who've got more to lose. They're yes-boys.

MRS Q. When they switch the Guinness to containers, that's the beginning of the end.

MAGICOTE. Right. It's not fair trade. How're we expected to tap into a container?

MRS Q. You can see that an awkward little dock like Bristol is going to be irrelevant.

CABBAGE. Is that what you can see, Mrs Q? In your tea-leaves?

MRS Q. Something like that.

WHIPPET. So what's the answer going to be?

MRS Q. A new dock down at Portbury, even bigger than Avonmouth. The Welsh ports will make a song and dance –

SONG. Sospan Fach …

MRS Q. – and it will wind up costing four times the estimate.

HAPPY PAPPY. And the Japanese will use it as a gurt car park.

MAGICOTE. Think of Avonmouth Docks when it was bustling and booming. And look at the robot atmosphere coming in now.

MRS Q. These container ships get turned round in a matter of hours. The sailors haven't got time for half a pint. They might as well be Martians.

RED BARON. There will be a determined move to get rid of the dockers that are in the docks. They'll phase out casual labour, but they'll still fiddle the rotas. Gradually they'll break us, in the name of rationalisation. Comradeship, workmanship, will be ships that pass in the night.

DOLLY. They'll offer redundancy terms that look generous to the older men, and the younger ones will just grab it without thinking.

MRS Q. Everyone in Lawrence Weston will have a new car.

RED BARON. Then they'll find they've got no docking force left and they'll ask us back. Not me.

WHIPPET. The small ships, what's to stop them still coming into Bristol? If they don't come here, where would they go?

DOLLY. They'd go to Sharpness. The dockers at Sharpness, well, they're cider drinkers. In summer they make hay. They casn't tell a strop from a snotter. They bring their dinner in a handbag.

HAPPY PAPPY. There's people, I'd call them criminals, who want to concrete over the docks, just to please motorists.

MRS Q. They'll stop spending the money on dredging, all we'll have left is a municipal duck pond. A water leisure facility.

CABBAGE. And the city centre, that'll be one big insurance office.

MRS Q. It's no use being nostalgic.

MAGICOTE. I'm not nostalgic. I just know what we've lost. It won't come back, and we can't go back. But you don't forget it. If you forget it, you'd wonder why Bristol's here at all.

WHIPPET. People won't forget it. How can they? It'll still be here, the harbour. It's not going to just be empty water, right in the middle of the city. Is it?

RED BARON. I promise you one thing, the shipyard will make a mint. They'll throw 300 men out of work, even though they're still profitable, sell their land for millions and get millions more in compensation. All stitched up in secret and never debated in the city council.

DOLLY. Do the people who run this city understand the first thing about the sea? Look at Neptune. For years, he's stuck near Temple Meads. At last it dawns on some bureaucrat he ought to be overlooking the port. They shift him there. Next thing, they take the ships away.

SONG. In Nineteen seventy-four
        Out through Hotwells Lock

55

An empty timber ship goes home.
Then they shut the dock.
CABBAGE. The rest is sand.
The CHANT *starts and continues to the end of the play.*
CHANT. Dicky-Bow Joe, Potty Trotter,
　　　Slippery Sam, Bamber Gascoigne ... *[Names continued at end.]*
DOLLY *(takes cutting from his wallet).* Did you see my farewell letter in
　　the paper? How it used to be, when I started. *(Reads.)* "Outside of
　　the main gate some 600 men stand around in groups. Most wear
　　flat caps with mufflers crosswise around their necks, the ends
　　tucked around their braces. A few wear straps round their legs to
　　keep their moleskin trousers from dragging the wet ground. A pall
　　of choking smoke from old clay pipes floats in the air. A hum of
　　conversation hushes as the stevedores mount the stand to call off
　　the banana boat. Everyone presses forward, and rushes in as soon
　　as their names are called. Among the crowd stands a youth of 19,
　　rather lost in the hubbub around him. His late father's black book
　　in his pocket and his old hook in his belt. He moves forward as
　　his name is called and thus began my first day as a registered dock
　　worker ... Now 42 years on, I have left my life around the screw.
　　I have no certificate on the wall, no watch in my pocket to thank
　　me for my services. All I possess is the memory of the many
　　comrades I worked with. Some good, some bad, but all stood as
　　one, right or wrong, in the struggles we had for a better standard
　　of living. This I am glad to see has now been achieved, but at the
　　expense of the mateyness and cheer that existed during my young
　　days; and the docks are a sadder place without it."
SONG. Prince Street, Prince Street,
　　They tore up the script and forgot the plot.
　　Inga, Neva,
　　Names once familiar as birds in the skies –
　　I can't see unless I close my eyes.

　　Prince Street, Prince Street,
　　Look at it now, what have you got?
　　Echoes, shadows,
　　Of a town people would not recognise –
　　I can't see unless I close my eyes.

　　Prince Street, Prince Street,

People who worked here never forgot.
They know, you know,
A tide that falls is a tide that will rise.
I can't see unless I close my eyes.
I can't see unless I close my eyes.

**

CHANT *(continued)*. Nail in the Boot, Lion Tamer,
Hobo and Omo and Emu and Moe –
Soft-talking Joe, Rack and Ruin,
Turkey Neck, Crazy Horse, Elbow.

Apple Face, Yellow Bird, Bonker,
Bent Nose, Porkie McPie,
Rachman, The Vicar, Cat Strangler,
Keynsham, Two Faces, Cod's Eye,

Poison Dwarf, Three Shots of Red Eye,
Bugger Me, Carry the Can,
The Jolly Green Giant, Bugs Waistcoat,
Sizzle Head, Rainwater Man,

The Hairdresser, Bread and Jam, Betty,
Still Life, The Sheriff, Straight Back,
Mechanical Man, Bonny Brighteyes,
Wishbone, The Slug, Jumping Jack,

Bucket Head, Nookie, White Hunter,
Man and a Half, Sailor Dick,
The Temperance Seven, Spud, Gandhi,
Milky Bar Kid, Evo Stick,

Spongehead, The Reject, Dog Teaser,
Crocodile Tears, Waste of Space,
Wrington Doughnut, Bald Eagle, Ant Eater,
Tubs, Egg on Legs, Rubber Face,

Whingeing Weasel, Lurch, Thumper, The Major,
Tadpoles, The Hanging Judge, Ego,
Mad Monk, Dr Strangelove, Storm Trooper,
Cuddles, O-Level, Geronimo,

No Neck, Shirley Temple, Romancer,

J. Arthur Rank, Baby Lee,
Donkey Head, Winky Woo, Tall Ships,
Elephant Boy, Mr Pastry,

Dragnet, Puffed Wheat, Father Christmas,
Smoking Croc, Dr Dolittle, Parrot,
Garth, Talking Horse, Cosy, Bunter,
Underpants, The Bionic Maggot,

Tower of Strength, Toby Jug, Glass Back,
Blender, Odd Legs, Silent Witness,
John Wayne, Grizzly Grabber, Tom Pepper,
K.O., Dick the Fly, Rigor Mortis,

The Ponce, Horace Bachelor, Lamb Chop,
Laughing Hyena, Pig's Ear,
Lord Charles, Badger's Arse, Puffing Billy,
Mickey Mouse, Verbal Diarrhoea,

Lickum and Stickum, Male Model,
Jim Crow, Pick a Pocket or Two,
Rupert the Bear, Preacher Williams,
Pound Note Face, Mr Magoo ...

THE COMPANY FOR THE PRODUCTION IN 2001

PRINCIPAL CHARACTERS IN ORDER OF APPEARANCE

SPOT	KATE MCNAB
MAGICOTE	ROSS HARVEY
DOLLY	FRED WEDLOCK
HAPPY PAPPY	HOWARD COGGINS
RED BARON	MARK BUFFERY
CABBAGE WATER	MARK MEADOWS
WHIPPET	STUART MCLOUGHLIN
HARRY	CHRISTIAN RODSKA
MRS Q	HEATHER WILLIAMS

SUPPORTING CAST

CRAZY HORSE	ROBIN BELFIELD
MAN IN A SUITCASE	BENJAMIN BIRD
RIGOR MORTIS	RICHARD BOND
SILENT WITNESS	RICHARD BROOKS
RUBBER FACE	ALAN CABLE
MUSCLES	JIM CUTIAND
THE DESTROYER	TERRY DUNBAR
SHIRLEY TEMPLE	TOBY FARROW
VERBAL DIARRHOEA	MARK GREGORY
NOOKIE	CHRIS HOLLIDAY
MALE MODEL	MARK HOLLIS
LAUGHING HYENA	DAVE HORSEMAN
MILKY BAR KID	MARTIN HOWARD
SOFT TALKING JOE	PETER LAING
THE WHITE WHALE	BRIAN MACEY
IMMACULATE GEORGE	EDDY MARTIN
WALKING WOOLWORTHS	MARTIN PARSONS
EVOSTICK	PAUL PEARSON
HAIRDRESSER	DAVID STEPHENSON
STILL LIFE	ANDREW STOCKER
BROKEN BOOMERANG	STEVEN TALBOT
THE PONCE	DARREN TURNOCK
OLYMPIC FLAME	SCOTT WALDREN
GANDHI	MARTIN WHATLEY

THE FEEDER BAND

WHISTLES/FLUTE/SAX	ROD SALTER
CONCERTINA/ACCORDION/KEYBOARDS	DAVE TOWNSEND
ELECTRIC AND ACOUSTIC GUITARS	KIT MORGAN
ELECTRIC AND ACOUSTIC BASS	DAVE GOODIER
DRUMS/PERCUSSION/KEYBOARDS	JOHN O'HARA

YOUTH THEATRE MEMBERS

BEN CARRUTHERS
JONATHAN HARES
ANDREW HAYNES
LEE JOHNSON
JOSEPH WALLACE
CHAPERONE   CHRIS DIBBLE

BRISTOL OLD VIC

DIRECTORS	GARETH MACHIN
	HEATHER WILLIAMS
SET & COSTUME DESIGNER	MICK BEARWISH
ORIGINAL MUSIC	JOHN O'HARA
PRODUCTION MANAGER	DEREK SIMPSON
LIGHTING DESIGNER	TIM STREADER
SOUND DESIGNER	JASON BARNES
STAGE MANAGER	JILL DAVEY
DEPUTY STAGE MANAGER	AMANDA ADAMS

BRISTOL MUSEUMS & ART GALLERY

CURATOR OF INDUSTRIAL AND MARITIME HISTORY	ANDY KING
RAILWAY OPERATIONS MANAGER	DAVE MARTIN
TUG MASTERS	ERNIE BLAKE
	COLIN TROTHAM
PILOT	PETER HODGE

BRISTOL CITY HARBOUR

CITY DOCKS GENERAL MANAGER	RICHARD SMITH
HARBOUR MANAGER	GEOFF LANE
SENIOR DUTY OFFICER	STEVE HEDGES
DOCK MASTER	BOB BIGWOOD
DEPUTY DOCK MASTER	BILL FOWLLEY
ALL HARBOUR OPERATIONS STAFF	

HOBBLERS
ROY RICE
ALBERT SHARP

CLASSIC TRANSPORT
LAWRENCE HAYWARD OF EMERALD TRAVEL

ARCHIVE FILM EDITOR
RUTH SIDERY

INDEPENDENT FILM MAKER
DEE RYDING

EDUCATION AND OUTREACH TEAM
TOBY HULSE
ANGIE HUNT
SALLY COOKSON

PUBLISHING LIAISON
PHIL GIBBY
ALISON FINN

*The original 1997 production
was devised by Andy Hay and A.C.H. Smith,
written by A.C.H. Smith, and directed by Andy Hay.*

BRISTOL OLD VIC COMPANY STAFF

EXECUTIVE DIRECTOR
SARAH SMITH
ASSOCIATE DIRECTOR
GARETH MACHIN
MUSICAL DIRECTOR
JOHN O'HARA
LITERARY ASSOCIATE
LUCY CATHERINE

RESIDENT PLAYWRIGHT
TOBY FARROW
ASSOCIATE WRITERS-IN-RESIDENCE
CATHERINE JOHNSON
KWAME KWEI-ARMAH
PA TO THE EXECUTIVE DIRECTOR
JUNE GADD

THEATRE FINANCIAL CONTROLLER
PHILIP EWINS
FINANCE ASSISTANT
DAVID RUMSEY
BAR & FRONT OF HOUSE ACCOUNTS SUPERVISOR
GERY WILDISH

EDUCATION AND YOUTH THEATRE

DIRECTOR
HEATHER WILLIAMS
ADMINISTRATOR
HILARY DAVIS

ASSISTANT DIRECTOR
TOBY HULSE
DESIGN ASSOCIATE
KATIE SYKES

ASSOCIATE ARTISTS
SALLY COOKSON
ANGIE HUNT

PRODUCTION

PRODUCTION MANAGER
DEREK SIMPSON
DEPUTY PRODUCTION MANAGER
JOANNA CUTHBERT
TECHNICAL MANAGER
FREDRICK STACEY
NEW VIC TECHNICIAN
CATHERINE CULLINANE
STAGE MANAGER
JILL DAVEY

DEPUTY STAGE MANAGER
AMANDA ADAMS
STAGE ASSISTANT
DAMIAN BUTLIN
STAGE MANAGEMENT PLACEMENTS
RIANON CHEFFERS-HEARD
HELEN SCOTT
GEMMA DOUGAN

HEAD FLYMAN
KEN SMITH
ASSISTANT FLYMAN
CHRIS KEEGAN
STAGE DAYMAN
JAMES THEARLE
COMPANY DRIVER
ROBERT CHAPPEL

DESIGN, PAINTING & PROPERTIES

HEAD OF DESIGN
MICK BEARWISH
HEAD SCENIC ARTIST
JANE COOKE
HEAD OF PROPS
PAUL BROWN
PROP MAKERS
BILL TALBOT
CELIA STRAINGE

PROP PLACEMENTS
DREW BAUMOHI
TIM DOUGHTY
LIGHTING & SOUND CHIEF ELECTRICIAN
TIM STREADER
DEPUTY CHIEF ELECTRICIAN
LORRAINE LAYBOURNE

DEPUTY ELECTRICIAN
JASON BARNES
ASSISTANT ELECTRICIAN
OLIVER HELLIS
FOLLOW SPOT OPERATOR
CHRISTIAN WALLACE

WORKSHOP

MASTER CARPENTER
SIMON LUCKWELL

DEPUTY MASTER CARPENTER
ANDY POWELL

CARPENTER
CHRISTOPHER CHAPMAN

WARDROBE

WARDROBE SUPERVISOR
JULIE HERBERT
MASTER TAILOR
TERRY MILTON

LADIES' CUTTER
CAROLINE REID-SINCLAIR
WARDROBE ASSISTANT
LYNNE MERRON

WARDROBE MAINTENANCE
KATHRYN BLIGHT
SKY CROSSINGHAM

HIRE DEPARTMENT

MANAGER
ANDRE CORDERY

MARKETING & DEVELOPMENT

DEVELOPMENT MANAGER
PHIL GIBBY
MARKETING OFFICER
ALISON FINN
AUDIENCE DEVELOPMENT OFFICER
MEGAN THOMAS

CUSTOMER LIAISON OFFICER
ANDREW STOCKER
GRAPHIC DESIGNER
NIALL ALLSOP
DISPLAY & GRAPHICS ASSISTANT
REBECCA SHEPPARD

DISTRIBUTION CO-ORDINATOR
JANE COHEN
DISTRIBUTION ASSISTANTS
ROGER ALDERTON
KEN JOHNSON

FRONT OF HOUSE

THEATRE MANAGER
ANTHONY ROLLE
DUTY HOUSE MANAGERS
CLARE DUNSTER
JEREMY FURBER
RHIANNON REID
SAMANTHA THOMPSON
BOX OFFICE SUPERVISOR
MEGAN SPARKS
SENIOR BOX OFFICE ASSISTANTS
CLARE DUNSTER
SIMON HARVEY-WILLIAMS

BOX OFFICE ASSISTANTS
LUCY MARTYN
JULIE WARRINGTON
STEPHEN WILLIAMS
CHEFS
FRAN WELBY
GEOFFREY KNEALE
CATERING ASSISTANTS
JUNE DAVIES
EMMA PARSLOW
KATH SCOTT

STAGE DOOR
VIVIENNE SWINDELLS
PHIL JOHN
MAINTENANCE
MIKE ELLIOTT
HOUSEKEEPER
BOB HOPES
CLEANERS
LINDA GOULD
ROSEMARY HOPES
BETTY HOOPER
INA RANKIN
PAUL TILEY

BOARD OF DIRECTORS

CHAIRMAN
DAVID SPROXTON
VICE-CHAIRMAN
JOHN SAVAGE
COMPANY SECRETARY
OVALSEC LTD

GOVERNORS
CATHERINE JOHNSON
LESLIE PERRIN
PAT ROBERTS
SIMON RELPH
CHRIS WILLMORE

ADVISORS
STEPHEN DILLEY
SOLOMON HARE
MALCOLM SHORNEY
STEPHEN WRAY
BRISTOL CITY COUNCIL
THEATRE CHAPLAIN
THE REVD CANON
NEVILLE BOUNDY

BRISTOL OLD VIC THEATRE SCHOOL

PRINCIPAL (AND ASSOCIATE DIRECTOR OF THE BRISTOL OLD VIC COMPANY)
CHRISTOPHER DENYS

BRISTOL COSTUME SERVICES LTD

PROPRIETOR
CATRIONA TYSON

THEATRE COLLECTION, UNIVERSITY OF BRISTOL

KEEPER
SARAH CUTHILL